THE FIRE INSIDE

THE DHARMA OF
JAMES BALDWIN AND AUDRE LORDE

RIMA VESELY-FLAD, PhD

North Atlantic Books
Huichin, unceded Ohlone land
Berkeley, California

North Atlantic Books
Huichin, unceded Ohlone land
2526 Martin Luther King Jr Way
Berkeley, CA 94704 USA
www.northatlanticbooks.com

Cover photo of Audre Lorde © Jack Mitchell via Getty Images, cover photo of James Baldwin © Rob Croes
Cover design by Amanda Weiss
Book design by Happenstance Type-O-Rama

Printed in the United States of America

The Fire Inside: The Dharma of James Baldwin and Audre Lorde is sponsored and published by North Atlantic Books, an educational nonprofit based in the unceded Ohlone land Huichin (Berkeley, CA) that collaborates with partners to develop cross-cultural perspectives; nurture holistic views of art, science, the humanities, and healing; and seed personal and global transformation by publishing work on the relationship of body, spirit, and nature.

Permissions for practices are listed at the end of this book on page 187.

North Atlantic Books's publications are distributed to the US trade and internationally by Penguin Random House Publisher Services. For further information, visit our website at www.northatlanticbooks.com.

Library of Congress Cataloging-in-Publication Data

Names: Vesely-Flad, Rima author
Title: The fire inside : the dharma of James Baldwin and Audre Lorde / Rima Vesley-Flad.
Description: Berkeley, California : North Atlantic Books, [2025] | Includes bibliographical references and index.
Identifiers: LCCN 2025003194 (print) | LCCN 2025003195 (ebook) | ISBN 9798889842583 trade paperback | ISBN 9798889842590 ebook
Subjects: LCSH: Baldwin, James, 1924-1987--Criticism and interpretation | Lorde, Audre--Criticism and interpretation | American literature--African American authors--History and criticism | American literature--20th century--History and criticism | Buddhist philosophy in literature | Buddhism in literature
Classification: LCC PS3552.A45 Z928 20225 (print) | LCC PS3552.A45 (ebook)
LC record available at https://lccn.loc.gov/2025003194
LC ebook record available at https://lccn.loc.gov/2025003195

The authorized representative in the EU for product safety and compliance is Eucomply OÜ, Pärnu mnt 139b-14, 11317 Tallinn, Estonia, hello@eucompliancepartner.com, +33757690241.

1 2 3 4 5 6 7 8 9 KPC 31 30 29 28 27 26

I dedicate this book to my ancestors:

Rev. Benjamin Harrison Gordon

Mallie Fox Gordon

Lucille Gordon Green

I celebrate being part of your lineage.

And they have begun to understand that if they are going to liberate themselves, they have to begin it first of all within themselves. No one is going to do it for them.

—JAMES BALDWIN, "SPEECH FROM THE SOLEDAD RALLY"

I am going to write fire until it comes out my ears, my eyes, my noseholes—everywhere. Until it's every breath I breathe.

—AUDRE LORDE, *A BURST OF LIGHT*

Contents

Introduction

James Baldwin wrote his first novel, *Go Tell It on the Mountain*, sitting on the bright red faux leather seats of Café de Flore. Decades later, I sat on those same seats and imagined Baldwin sinking into memories of his childhood as he wrote, making sense of his early experiences as he stared at the fan-like tile pattern on the floor, the fake red and white flowers in tall, narrow vases. I could see him staring at the mirrors on the wall and seeing his own reflection, taking note of the features that had been cruelly mocked in his youth. I envisioned him remembering the man he called his father.

"Everyone had always said that John would be a preacher when he grew up, just like his father," Baldwin wrote.[1] It is the first line of Baldwin's novel, which he acknowledged is autobiographical in nature. In the novel, Baldwin, through the voice of a young man named John, yearns for love, a love that he will never receive from his father. He commits to the church, but this too does not bring the love he expects.

Baldwin, through his writing of John, went into his suffering: the experience of being despised by his stepfather—the man he called his father—and the white world. Then he envisioned another father—imagined, biological—both for John and for himself. This father was not a preacher; he did not even believe in God. Richard, John's father, smokes and cusses. He loves science, art, and history museums.[2] This imagined father evokes Baldwin's own love for learning. As Baldwin himself said, it was his teachers' early recognition of his intelligence that would save him, that would help him save himself.

Baldwin saved himself by turning toward his pain. He published *Nobody Knows My Name* in 1961. It is the title of a collection of essays about race and racism, exile and belonging. His later book *No Name in the Street* (1972) unraveled the absences that he had endured throughout his lifetime. Absence was a central theme for Audre Lorde, too. She wrote extensively about alienation from her family of origin, of experiencing her parents and sisters as distant and cold. She only found affection within her family in her final years, with one of her half-sisters as Lorde battled liver cancer. Her father's three other children had lived in the Caribbean; she had not known of their existence until very late in life. But absence did not have the last word. In 1982 Audre Lorde published *Zami: A New Spelling of My Name.* For Lorde and Baldwin, writing became a way to turn to absences and establish a presence, in their own language, on their own terms.

The experience of self-creation born of estrangement—what Audre Lorde described as the wisdom arising from living as a "sister outsider"—would shape her awareness of herself and her relationships with other Black women over decades. So, too, would Lorde's physical presence in the world. She was legally blind and did not speak until the age of four, but she embraced these seeming disabilities as gifts that fostered her enormous vision—the capacity to see differently and to dream, to honor difference, to articulate herself through poetry. In her adult life, she wrote about the complicated dynamics she experienced with Black women with unflinching honesty.

Anguish mingled with tenderness. As I sat in Café de Flore, and later, as I stood in front of Paris's most esteemed university, the Sorbonne, I was attuned to Lorde's fierce power, to Baldwin's unflinching capacity to see into himself and to look directly at the world around him. "All you are ever told in this country about being black is that it is a terrible, terrible thing to be," Baldwin stated in 1961. "Now, in order to survive this, you have to really dig down into yourself and re-create yourself, really, according to no image which yet exists in America . . . you have to *decide* who you are, and force the world to deal with you, not with its *idea* of you."[3] I heard Baldwin. I heard Lorde say the same thing, in her own way, time and again. They were unshakable, protective. I was increasingly aware of what it had taken for them to attain such strength. Like them, I had come up against a rigid, conservative theology in my home; I, too, had been hated by members of my family. I had been abandoned by my father and completely cut off from his lineage. For nearly five decades, I did not know my paternal grandmother's name. I knew what absence meant. Yet, through books, I had learned to imagine something else: another way of being, another world to live in. I resonated with Baldwin and Lorde's love for words. I was a lover of ideas, theories, language—of literature and poetry. I, too, was determined to re-create myself.

I saw myself as capable. But I did not see myself as powerful and fierce. I reckoned with my penchant for self-silencing; I was wired to make myself safe. But I was inspired by Baldwin and Lorde to face my own suffering—the absences, the hatred—and perhaps in doing so, to cultivate a deep sense of authority within my own being.

Their writing provided a way forward. Audre Lorde spoke of the mother warrior poet: tender and protective. I could not envision an imagined father, as Baldwin had, but I could conceive of a watchful, vigilant maternal figure. She assumed a form in my mind that mirrored rolling hills, rippling water. Mother Yemanjá. Yoruba legend spoke of rivers that flowed from her breasts. She provided safety and nourishment. She was capable of enacting volcanoes and earthquakes.

I thought of the support offered by Mother Earth to the historical Buddha when I attuned to Lorde's embrace of the mother-goddess. Legend tells us that the historical Buddha touched Mother Earth for support on the night he was enlightened. His mind was attacked from all directions, but he sat still and summoned the strength of maternal bedrock. She responded as a witness to his accomplishment. The stories of the Buddha encouraged me to believe in my capacity to turn toward my suffering and to be liberated from it, *with support*. This, for me, was power. Buddhist teachers encouraged me to trust my experience. I learned practices for working skillfully with my pain, training my mind on how to stay with everything that arose: internalized messages, physical aches. This was hard work. I was inspired by the Asian and Asian-American monastics whose practical and spiritual labor brought forward the teachings over 2,600 years. The teachings were transmitted to me, too, by Black Buddhists—many of whom are quoted in this book—who modeled a practice of attaining inner stability. I saw in their example a sustained strength, a deep compassion.

Before that I was so often a wreck. Insecure. Overwhelmed. Struggling to respond to the forces of racism around me. Compelled to respond to suffering—my own and others—with very few resources.

And yet. There were maps. I knew this from Buddhist teachings. I absorbed this from the writings of Baldwin and Lorde. In Paris, standing in front of the Sorbonne, I felt my heart open. A couple was dancing the tango in the square. There was joy in the air. I walked to the entrance doors of the massive stone building. It represented the origins of ideas, the power of thoughts and words. I sought to carry that power forward in my own life, to honor the lineages of Black, queer luminaries and of Buddhist teachers who had informed my own practices of liberation.

· · ·

This book is a testament to the messages of freedom in Baldwin, Lorde, and the Buddha. It is also a statement of the ways in which my meditation practice moved from my own inward healing to outward action.

I have resonated with Buddhism on a gut level. At the same time, the forms of Buddhism I originally learned did not directly address state violence. I have needed to learn how my tradition informs my ethical actions and to find other Buddhists who are equally committed to dismantling violent institutions.

If Black Radical writers have urged me to decolonize my mind, Buddhist teachings and practices have provided a salient, clear way to do it. But it is a cyclical process. We cannot only be focused on internal liberation. We are compelled to change oppressive conditions that lead to suffering, too. As I have learned to heal my heart and mind, I have continued to confront violent, oppressive power: policing, occupation, ethnic cleansing, and genocide. There is a global war against people like me—unwanted, except for extractive labor—by nations with extraordinary military power and, increasingly, militarized AI weapons. We are deemed polluted and disposable. We are subjected to overwhelming violence even as we are fed degrading narratives.

This has been strikingly, immediately evident in the genocide and ethnic cleansing of Palestinians.

As I have been writing this manuscript, I have been deeply attuned to the suffering of Palestinians in Gaza and the West Bank. How do we meet the magnitude of this suffering, of Palestinians as well as our own? How do we nuance the fraught political and religious dynamics of the situation without reducing its complexity into polarized schools of thought? Baldwin, Lorde, and the Buddhist teachings have provided a way forward for me—as has my community. The coming together of these different streams comprises the material in this book.

As I conclude the writing of this manuscript, I have just broken bread and engaged in rituals with activists of different religious traditions, including Buddhism, to cultivate a sense of collective grounding as we support Palestinians who are under attack. In an effort to share some of the practical ways we have engaged to metabolize suffering and act from a grounded place, I have included at the end of each chapter practices offered by Black Buddhist teachers of different lineages.

May these words—of James Baldwin and Audre Lorde, of the Buddha and Black Buddhist teachers—inspire you. May we, individually and collectively, transform the painful conditioning of our minds as we work to transform the violent conditions of our world.

The Transformation of Silence into Language and Action

Bile, phlegm, and also wind,

Imbalance and climate too,

Carelessness and assault,

With kamma result as the eighth.

—MOLIYASIVAKA SUTTA

I am compelled to stand with those who, due to oppressive conditions, are silenced in the halls of power.

This is not always easy. I grew up in an environment in which I learned to self-silence, to perform for attention and affection, to refrain from speaking directly. I wrote in journals, but these were private thoughts, meant only for my own eyes. In college, as a reporter, and later, as an academic, I often hid behind the words and analyses of others; I preferred to quote them rather than use my own voice. I was afraid to speak out for fear of being ostracized again, after being exiled from my family of origin. Exile had been my defining experience from the moment I was born.

"And of course I am afraid," wrote Audre Lorde in 1977, "because the transformation of silence into language and action is an act of self-revelation, and that always seems fraught with danger."[1] This fear of speaking directly, for fear of being exiled or of harming others, arises from self-doubt that remains submerged unless I give it space to breathe. But it is also a fear of being hurt, an awareness of lack of safety, a sense of impending exile. I am present with it all. But I am also compelled to speak with others, as I wanted protectors to stand up for me. I stand in the lineage of Audre Lorde: I acknowledge my desire for safety, and I risk exile in order to advocate for others.

In my youth, I had a few protectors whom I called "mother figures." Even as I grew up estranged from my family of origin, these were women who loved me with fierce tenderness. I had two godmothers, one of whom claimed me as her goddaughter when I was ten. She was a Jewish woman, born in France; she came of age as Hitler's Third Reich gained power and conquered neighboring nations. Her father, a famous filmmaker, and her mother were offered asylum in the United States. But they were not allowed to bring their only daughter, my godmother. They placed her in a Catholic convent and fled. She, in turn, suffered horrific anti-Semitic abuse within the convent, where, as a Jewish girl, she was blamed for the Nazi occupation of France. Years later, after the war, she was sent to the United States to reunite with her parents. The horror of persecution never left her. When she arrived in the US, she renamed herself and buried deeply the trauma that she had experienced.

I start this chapter with my fear of speaking and my godmother's story because I vacillate between empathy and rage. I am writing in real time, as a genocide is taking place in Gaza and ethnic cleansing is occurring with the full backing of the United States, with my tax dollars. I am compelled to speak. And I seek practices within the Buddhist tradition to work skillfully with the depth of my empathy and rage. These feelings are constantly arising, constantly in tension. So too are the impulses to be safe and to protect. I seek to hold it all at once, without reacting and without self-silencing. The trauma being unleashed on Palestinians is triggering my own ancestral trauma. I am sensitive, too, to the trauma unleashed under Nazi reign, and the desire for safety and security that is embedded in the cells of Jewish survivors and their descendants. When I researched biological manifestations of intergenerational trauma for my second book, the studies I read on how trauma impacts cellular changes were studies of Jewish families. I was—and am—able to acknowledge how trauma and fear result from collective racial violence, over decades and centuries. I can see it in my own life.

And yet I am overwhelmed with rage, daily, as I watch the horrors of the genocide in Gaza and my inbox and social media feeds fill with images of ethnic cleansing in the West Bank. I have no words to express the level of grief that I feel. I identify deeply with the suffering I witness; it evokes centuries of horror inflicted upon Black bodies, even as it occurs in a different place, on a different scale. And more, I am filled with anger as pro-Israel lobbying organizations spend millions of dollars to unseat progressive Black congressional representatives, and when billionaires use their wealth to take down prominent Black academics and silence pro-Palestinian activists. I hold my empathy and my rage together. I seek to honor the continuum between them. To balance all that arises, I strive to put myself into close proximity to people whose nuanced understandings of the dynamics between Israel and Palestine, the United States and Israel, and Black and Jewish peoples in the United States challenge assumptions and stereotypes.

It requires great intention and emotional labor. It requires time.

But this is my karma. I think of this intention—to cultivate awareness, to speak deliberately, and to act skillfully—as my work in the world. And in my fear, in my desire to protect myself, I hear echoes of Audre Lorde's poetry. She expressed her fear of speaking out. And yet. She refused to stay silent.

In her poem, "A Litany for Survival," Lorde speaks to "those of us / who were imprinted with fear." She points out that fear is wielded as a "weapon," that we internalize an "illusion of some safety to be found." Authorities seek to silence us. Consequently, we self-silence. We internalize the fear that we will not be heard "nor welcome" and repress our voices ourselves. But she acknowledges, "when we are silent / we are still afraid." Therefore, she reminds us, "it is better to speak / remembering / we were never meant to survive."[2]

Nowhere has my own fear arisen more than in speaking out in 2024 against the genocide in Gaza. The word "anti-Semitic" is a label leveled at anyone who challenges the actions of the state of Israel. Scholar Benjamin Sax writes that being called anti-Semitic is like being labeled a Nazi.[3] I feel that in my bones. Even as my political community boldly confronts the state of Israel's aggression against Palestinians, I find myself puzzling over how to talk about the genocide in Buddhist communities where there is overwhelming, oppressive silence.[4] I risk emotional safety, exile, cancellation if I speak out. I fear creating more harm.

And yet, to not speak on behalf of Palestinian suffering is to betray my community. It is to betray myself. "We can sit in our corners mute forever while our sisters and our selves are wasted, while our children are distorted and destroyed, while our earth is poisoned; we can sit in our safe corners mute as bottles, and we will still be no less afraid," Lorde wrote.[5]

This is a point of practice for me. I turn to the *suttas*. I turn to Audre Lorde, again and again. I turn to James Baldwin.

Baldwin on Israel

Baldwin was sensitive to the suffering of European Jews who had survived the Holocaust and Arabs who were displaced as a result of the United Nations declaration (Resolution 181), which divided formerly British-ruled Mandatory Palestine into Arab Palestinian territory and

Jewish territory (the latter of which formed as a nation-state in 1948). He wrote about Israel and Palestine over several decades, starting in 1961. He made clear: His rejection of an ethnonationalist Jewish state was not a rejection of Jews, despite his childhood experiences of exploitative Jewish landlords and shop owners in Harlem. He abhorred the settler colonialism he experienced in Israel just thirteen years after it was established as a nation-state. At the same time, he detested the racism embedded in anti-Semitism. He was well aware of the disproportionate influence of Jewish thinkers, writers, and artists in social justice movements in the US, and the compassion shown by Jewish people toward the suffering of Black people. Baldwin's best friend and many of his classmates in high school were Jewish, a fact that provoked lengthy reflection by Baldwin, who wrote in *The Fire Next Time* that he "could find no point of connection between them and the Jewish pawnbrokers and landlords and grocery-store owners in Harlem."[6] Baldwin defended his best friend to his stepfather—who expressed anti-Semitism—as "a better Christian than you are."[7] During the civil rights movement, Baldwin moved in multiracial circles, which were well attended and supported by Jewish activists.

But two shifts in Baldwin's life expanded his worldview with regard to the ethnonationalist Jewish state. In one shift, he visited the state of Israel as an invited guest. Initially he was supportive of the state of Israel; he was escorted to many notable, historical places and treated well by his hosts. But he observed, continuously, that "you can't walk five minutes without finding yourself at a border."[8] He took note, attentively, intuitively, of the ways in which Palestinians were treated and found numerous corollaries with the oppression of Black Americans. He could not be at ease. "I don't believe that they [Jews] have the right, after three thousand years, to reclaim the land with Western bombs and guns on Biblical injunction," Baldwin reflected in a 1970 interview. "When I was in Israel it was as though I was in the middle of *The Fire Next Time*."[9]

The 1961 visit to Israel was ultimately so unnerving that, rather than go to Africa, as planned, Baldwin went to Turkey. He felt that while traveling through Africa, he would be overwhelmed by the fact of European colonialism, whereas in Turkey—a country to which he would return time and again over the following decade—he had spaciousness to process the manifestations of colonialism. In Turkey, he mulled over his experience of Israel, concluding that the new nation-state mirrored the racist structures of the United States in distinct and obvious ways.[10]

Following his trip to Israel, Baldwin embraced the worldview that soon became associated with the Black Power movement. He was among several notable intellectual peers as his own perspectives evolved: Martin Luther King Jr. visited Palestine and Israel in 1959; Malcolm X visited Cairo and Gaza during his 1964 pilgrimage.[11] Baldwin's visit, and his resulting alienation from the nation-state of Israel, would reverberate within the widening influence of the Black Power movement.

I listened to Baldwin's willingness to confront the racist violence embedded in the existence of Israel. Baldwin framed his opposition to the ethnonationalist state as a rejection of settler colonialism, which he associated with political Zionism. He rejected conflating anti-Semitism with anti-Zionism: "I am not anti-Semitic at all, but I am anti-Zionist," he stated numerous times.[12]

Baldwin repeatedly pointed out the contradictions inherent in the formation of the state of Israel. He acknowledged with empathy the horrors enacted upon Jews by Europeans during the *Shoah* (Holocaust). He recognized that the drive for a Jewish state arose from a depth of suffering: the genocide committed during the Holocaust and pogroms over centuries. And he pointed to a continuing pattern of white, Christian exploitation of Jews.

> But the state of Israel was not created for the salvation of the Jews; it was created for the salvation of the Western interests. This is what is becoming clear (I must say that it was always clear to me). The Palestinians have been paying for

the British colonial policy of "divide and rule" and for Europe's guilty Christian conscience for more than thirty years.[13]

Yet none of these horrors absolved Jewish people of their responsibility to act ethically. If anything, Baldwin believed, such horrors should prompt Jewish Israelis to refrain from committing the same horrors of expulsion and ethnic cleansing that they had themselves experienced. Baldwin took note of the Israeli refusal to create a sovereign nation-state for Palestinians, even though the founding of an independent Palestinian state was mandated in the UN charter that allowed for the existence of Israel. He knew that there could not be peace in the Middle East until Palestinians possessed collective agency, sovereignty, and self-determination.

It was incumbent, then, on the newly formed state of Israel in historic Mandatory Palestine to not, in turn, carry out ethnic cleansing and genocide against Arab and Muslim peoples. But Baldwin was not ignorant of the political drive for the consolidation of power. He pointed out that in the creation of an ethnonationalist Jewish state in 1948, Jewish soldiers expelled more than seven hundred thousand Palestinians from their homes and drove them into refugee camps in Gaza and the West Bank. Palestinians call this the *Nakba* (Catastrophe).

Baldwin, moreover, held the state of Israel accountable for its part in supporting white minority rule through its selling of arms to the apartheid government of South Africa, which implemented a brutal, oppressive system of racial segregation in a nation that was 87 percent Black.[14]

He held the violations of the Israeli state in tension with the Jewish desire for safety. As a Black American, he understood intergenerational trauma, and its consequent fear, in his bones. But safety could not arise from committing mass violence against another people or theft by stealing the land belonging to that people; nor could it justify the expulsion and oppression of Palestinians.

Like others in the Black Power movement, Baldwin identified US support for Israel as an extension of Western domination. It was critical for him to name the power dynamics of Western colonialism and to speak out against the multiple forms of racism he observed. He noted that European-descended Israelis oppressed fellow Israelis of color. More than half of Israelis had moved to Israel from Arab and African states in which they experienced oppression. And yet, in Israel, white supremacist racial hierarchies were still entrenched. In Israel, Baldwin observed, European-descended Jews retained social and political positions of power, and Middle Eastern and African Jews were seen as inferior.[15]

The Doctrine of Karma

Baldwin was concerned with the structure of power in the world and in the US, particularly the dominant role that the US played in the wake of World War II. It is this concern with power that can be understood through the Buddhist teaching of karma.

There are varied, contested understandings of the doctrine of karma. The classical Buddhist understanding is that karma is intentional action; it includes thoughts, words, and deeds that are impacted by actions in a previous lifetime.[16] This interpretation posits that a person's present conditions are a result of behavior (poor or honorable) in past lives. It is an idea that has often been weaponized against oppressed groups that are deemed worthy of subjugation; certain schools of thought propose that low social status is the result of bad actions in previous lifetimes.[17]

The *Moliyasivaka Sutta* quoted at the beginning of this chapter offers a different interpretation by the Buddha. When the Buddha is asked whether he accepts the view that all suffering and all pleasure are caused by previous deeds, he replies that physical illnesses and physical conditions also play a role. Karma is the "eighth" reason given for the experience of pain and/or pleasure.

The Buddha *does* argue that our present conditions are informed by our past conduct. *Karma* (in Pali, *kamma*) is a Sanskrit term that is intimately connected to the Pali term *sankhara*, which refers to ingrained, volitional, mental patterns. We inherit ways of responding to our environment. I find this idea personally compelling, in that it helps me look at psychological patterns that do not serve my own personal well-being.

Yet we are not fixed beings: in the concept of *anatta*, or Not Self—of which *sankhara* forms one part—the Buddha argued that human beings are themselves impermanent. Volitional patterns are ingrained but flexible; ultimately, humans can be liberated from them. With attention to our thoughts, words, and deeds, human beings can be free of our deeply embedded habits.

In short, the doctrine of karma teaches that, through mindfulness, we can see how we are wired in response to our environment and can change our habitual reactions.

Furthermore, Buddhism teaches that we are not just individual islands; we are interconnected. This idea points to a theory of collective karma. A theory of collective karma argues that conditions, collective ideas, and social dynamics influence individual karma. This is to say: We are indebted to collective ideas before we know language. Thinking produces karma; logical reasoning relies on words.[18] Through language and other creative endeavors, we collectively produce culture. Our habit formations are not just individual, but also continued cultural practices and products: the creativity in the mind projected onto our shared environments.[19] And as beings with bodies, feelings, and consciousness, we are always responding to our conditions. As a result, our individual selves—including all that we have inherited, our minds and bodily senses—are always working in response to our natural and human environments. We are interdependent with all things. We are constantly responding to causes and conditions. The consequences of our responsive thoughts, words, and deeds are part of collective karma.[20]

In other words, an individual's actions are not solely responsible for their karma because an individual is always responding to collective conditions. At the same time, an individual can become aware of their thoughts, words, and actions and can intentionally change them to bring about greater well-being.[21]

Our lives are intimately connected to other people's lives—not only to our immediate families and communities, but also to future generations. The Buddha taught that it is critically important to understand how our individual actions can impact our present lives, as well as the next life and future lives that we cannot foresee. Actions, words, and thoughts have long consequences that "proceed forward, from life to life, generation to generation."[22]

The Sri Lankan scholar Nalin Swaris, who took a socio-historical approach to Buddhism, argued that the doctrine of karma contains seeds for personal as well as social liberation.[23] He, like other contemporary Buddhist activists, was deeply indebted to Western philosophy as well as Buddhist tradition. He took into account conditions such as poverty and war, as well as collective values and belief systems, as root causes of suffering. These belief systems are perpetuated in ideas and images that become normalized over generations and are projected in social institutions such as schools and religious communities.[24]

Swaris lifted up the Buddhist principle of impermanence—including of the human person—as liberatory. We, and our environments, are constantly in process. We inherit language, ideas, relationships, and institutions, but we are also actors. We have agency.

Swaris argued that in Buddhism, the idea of collective karma is intimately linked to the doctrine of "co-arising." When one thing arises, another arises in response; when one person or group acts, it engenders a reaction. This is important because, by extension, the Buddhist doctrine of co-arising tells us that the social conditions that drive certain aspects of suffering *can* be reversed. Our thoughts, words, and deeds—our karma—can influence our conditions.

Swaris argued that "to understand karma as collective action is to understand the necessity of collective action for freedom."[25] Humans find themselves in circumstances not of their choosing, but *they can change those circumstances* by understanding the nature of their conditions, as well as the nature of impermanence and co-arising.

Baldwin on Black-Jewish Dynamics in the US

Swaris, as a Buddhist, was fundamentally optimistic. So was Baldwin. In the 1960s, Baldwin committed himself to the civil rights movement and the Black Power movement, and sought to change the conditions that led to unnecessary suffering. He continued to engage in foreign policy analysis even as he took on racism and exploitation in the US context.

Baldwin extended his critique of Christian exploitation of Israel to the dynamics between Black people and Jewish people. Parsing this complicated set of relationships was part of a broader acknowledgment of the structures of power. As he did in 1961 when observing settler colonialism in Israel, in a 1967 *New York Times* article "Negroes Are Anti-Semitic Because They're Anti-White," Baldwin described the conflation of whiteness and Christianity, noting how the doctrines and institutions of the church undergird and perpetuate white supremacy.[26]

His analysis of the complicated relationships between Black and Jewish people arose from three vantage points. He remembered well the meaning of the Biblical Exodus narrative for Black church members who related the enslavement of Israelites to the bondage of their ancestors. He noted the experience of exploitation of Black people living in Harlem, who were taken advantage of by Jewish landlords, shop keepers, butchers, and grocers. And, he highlighted his friendships with Jewish classmates from his high school years; some of these relationships would be lifelong.

From these three defining experiences with Jews in the United States, Baldwin addressed the complicated relationships between Black and Jewish people more broadly. He argued that Jews—regardless of how they self-identify and how they experience intra-Jewish hierarchies—assimilate into whiteness. Baldwin did not address Jews of color; for Baldwin, Jews, in the minds of Black people, are white. Regardless of shared narratives of enslavement, Baldwin said, anti-Semitism and anti-Black racism are not the same.[27]

Baldwin directly acknowledged a power dynamic into which Jews had assimilated, intentionally or unintentionally. "The only thing white people have that black people need, or should want, is power—and no one holds power forever," he wrote.[28] Jews—like Irish Catholics and Eastern Europeans—were *able* to become white.[29] Moreover, Jews became the face of whiteness in Harlem. Regardless of how they saw themselves, Jews in the United States participated in a white-Black power dichotomy in which white people defined themselves over and against Blackness.

Baldwin analyzed how the Jewish-Black power dynamic mapped onto a white-Black power structure.

> In the American context, the most ironical thing about Negro anti-Semitism is that the Negro is really condemning the Jew for having become an American white man—for having become, in effect, a Christian. The Jew profits from his status in America, and he must expect Negroes to distrust him for it. The Jew does not realize that the credential he offers, the fact that he has been despised and slaughtered, does not increase the Negro's understanding. It increases the Negro's rage.[30]

One aspect of this rage was about being exploited by Jews; yet another was the double standard applied to Jews, whose violence in Israel was celebrated. Baldwin was cognizant that Black people supporting violent political action—including conquest, as Israel had done—would be crushed by militarized US forces. But Jews were given a pass as whites whose violence was legitimized. "The Jew is a white man, and when white men rise up against oppression, they are heroes: when black men rise, they have reverted to their native savagery," Baldwin wrote.[31]

Yet the dynamic was still more complicated for Baldwin. He charged that Jewish violence is celebrated in part because Jews are exploited by Christian institutions. The Christian world, which believes that it has supplanted Jews as God's chosen people, perpetuates not only a psychological narrative of white Christian superiority; it also requires that the Jew does Christians' "dirty work" in Harlem.[32] He reiterated these words in 1979: "Well. The Jew, in America, is a white man. He has to be, since I am a black man, and, as he supposes, his only protection against the fate which drove him to America. But he is still doing the Christian's dirty work, and black men know it."[33]

In a conversation with several other thinkers, scholar Marc Lamont Hill theorizes: "The image of the Jew, for Baldwin, is singled out by Negroes not because he acts differently from other white men, but because he doesn't."[34]

It is incumbent upon Jewish people, Baldwin charged, to see clearly their position of white privilege and to change their patterns of exploitation of Black people. Ultimately, Baldwin said, it is critical to name the white, Christian power structure around which Jews and Black people constantly revolve. Black people should strive to see the broader conditions in which anti-Semitism exists. And in the same way that Baldwin exhorted Black people to not buy into myths—as white Christians had done, and as he saw Black Christians and Muslims doing—he exhorted Black people to not perpetuate anti-Semitism, and instead see the exploitation of Jews as part of a larger pattern.

Baldwin indicted Jewish people for their racism against Black people. But he discouraged Black people from jumping on the anti-Semitic bandwagon. "I also know that if today I refuse to hate Jews, or anybody else, it is because I know how it feels to be hated,"[35] Baldwin wrote.

The practice, then, individually and collectively, is to see clearly the power structure at work. In order to change dynamics within the power structure, the racialized, religious foundations have to be acknowledged: "The crisis taking place in the world, and in the minds and hearts of black men everywhere, is not produced by the star of David, but by the old, rugged Roman cross on which Christendom's most celebrated Jew was murdered. And not by Jews," Baldwin stated.[36]

To see power dynamics and to refuse to perpetuate white, Christian supremacist ideas—including internalizing anti-Semitism—was an ethical imperative for Baldwin. I sat with his analysis. But *how* was I to practice within it, especially when images of the genocide in Gaza and news of ethnic cleansing flooded my inbox constantly? I was so often filled with grief and hatred. This is where I turned to the doctrine of karma.

Right Speech and Right Action: Acknowledging Power Dynamics

I have come to believe over and over again that what is most important to me must be spoken, made verbal and shared, even at the risk of having it bruised or misunderstood . . . And of course I am afraid, because the transformation of silence into language and action is an act of self-revelation, and that always seems fraught with danger.

—AUDRE LORDE, IN *SISTER OUTSIDER*

"Of course I am afraid," Audre Lorde wrote. To speak is to invite danger, to risk being misunderstood, to risk alienation or cancellation. I am afraid to speak at the risk of being heard as anti-Semitic. This was a risk that Baldwin took, too.

At the same time, to stay silent is to remain complicit. We all participate in collective karma, Swaris argued. He is among a number of Buddhist scholars who posit that Right Thought and Right Speech arise from acknowledging injustices and power dynamics, and being willing to acknowledge the nuances of oppression.[37] Right Action must address the harm of expulsion and occupation.

The refusal to stay silent prompted Zen Buddhist monk Thich Nhat Hanh to speak out against the devastation of the American war in Vietnam. In 1967, Nhat Hanh wrote a public letter to Martin Luther King Jr. in which he stated: "The great world humanists cannot remain silent. You yourself cannot remain silent."[38] And King spoke. His stance against the war in Vietnam was unpopular; he risked losing support from federal government leaders, particularly Lyndon B. Johnson, who had signed into law the Civil Rights Act of 1964 and the Voting Rights Act of 1965. But King acknowledged the contradictions between the unjustifiable slaughter of peasants in the war in Vietnam and his non-violent Christian ethics; between the unjustifiable billions of dollars spent to commit atrocities overseas and the perpetuation of poverty in the United States.[39]

Nhat Hanh, through a Buddhist lens, and King, through a Christian lens, saw that oppressive violence does not make the world safer. They spoke out against it as a practice of Right Speech, acknowledging the sources of suffering, including the reality of state violence. In her Introduction to Nhat Hanh's *Peace Begins Here: Palestinians and Israelis Listening to Each Other*, Sister Thai Nghiem wrote:

> We can start by expressing clearly that no act of violence or oppression has ever brought peace or happiness to anyone, neither the oppressed nor the oppressor. We should not be afraid to take a clear stand. But if, while taking a clear stand, we find ourselves excluding any of our human brothers and sisters—whoever they may be and whatever party or nationality they may belong to—then we have already failed in our efforts to live in peace. No one should be excluded from our peace process.[40]

And the doctrine of karma is particularly relevant in this context. It states that our thoughts, words, and deeds have implications.

The doctrine of karma offers a worldview and practices. We are taught to work with our minds and bodies; we are taught to turn

toward suffering and know it intimately. But this capacity to face suffering is larger than our individual selves; the focus on interior life
cannot feed silence and complicity in the midst of the violence of
occupation, apartheid, and colonialism. The struggle to free Palestine
from the horrors of the Israeli occupation and genocide is a struggle
intertwined with every freedom movement around the globe, including the struggle to decolonize our minds.

Many Buddhists alarmed by the genocide in Gaza advocate cultivating compassion.[41] This is a point of practice. It is hard for me
to cultivate compassion for violent settlers raiding and setting fire
to Palestinian lands with impunity. Such actions do not just come
from a place of trauma; they also arise from a messianic belief that
Palestinian land belongs to the state of Israel. How do I see this
clearly without devolving into intense hatred? Thoughts have consequences, too.

I draw analogies between what is happening in Gaza and the West
Bank and nineteenth-century white Southerners bent on holding
up the system of segregation—the legal structures, the social norms,
the humiliations—that functioned on the premise that Black people
are inferior to whites. It is hard to not hate people who reify such a
belief. I understand more of what Baldwin acknowledged when he
saw white Southerners' violence and pitied their narrow-mindedness,
their limitations.

"People who shut their eyes to reality simply invite their own
destruction, and anyone who insists on remaining in a state of innocence long after that innocence is dead turns himself into a monster,"
Baldwin wrote.[42] He was talking about the ways in which delusion
and avoidance operate in white communities worldwide, including
in the United States. He was in Switzerland when he wrote the essay
"Stranger in the Village," but he could have been talking about Jewish
Israeli settlers, who espouse the desire to annex Palestinian land and
support a right-wing government that refuses to consider a Palestinian

state. Their solution to the existence of Palestinians is to tighten controls and drive them out, violently.

Sectors of the Israeli public appear to go along with the idea that all Palestinians can be controlled if Israeli machinery is sophisticated enough. Supporters of the right-wing government who illegally built settlements refuse to recognize the humanity of Palestinians and their ancestral claim to the land. For many, this avoidance is rooted in Biblical interpretation. Baldwin's words ring true every time I read yet another article announcing curbs on the Israeli press, the dismantling of a "democracy" by changing the system of judicial checks and balances, and the maintenance of an apartheid system of separate roads, communities, and institutions built by Israelis on Palestinian land. Jewish Israelis do not—can choose not to—see what the rest of the world can see: the value of Palestinian life amidst the horrors of ethnic cleansing and genocide. Many critical Israelis attribute this "apathy" to willful blindness resulting from manipulative messaging of the right-wing Israeli government.[43]

As the genocide unfolded in 2024, and has unfolded in 2025 at the time of concluding this book, Baldwin's words have never seemed so prescient. Certainly, there is tremendous fear within Israel—of annihilation, of the collapse of the state. The atrocities of October 7, 2023, brought Israelis' worst fears into reality: mass, indiscriminate slaughter of civilians, including children. And then the refusal of the right-wing prime minister, Benjamin Netanyahu, to negotiate release of the hostages that remain in Gaza has perpetuated Jewish trauma. Jewish Israelis are mired in fear, unable to hold the hostile forces of their government accountable, unwilling to see the destruction that their government perpetuates.

But I, like many other Black Americans, like South West Asian and North African Buddhists, observe that violent oppression of Palestinians can never bring safety and security to Jewish Israelis. And as a Buddhist practitioner, it is important for me to speak out against the violence sanctioned by my government, my tax dollars. The policies of the US government do not represent my commitments. I am horrified by the massacres in Gaza, day after day, by the constant terrorizing of Palestinians in the West Bank. I think daily of Baldwin's words: "You don't know what's happening on the other side of the wall, because you don't want to know."[44] Most Israelis do not acknowledge the genocide, the use of famine as a weapon of war. But the world is outraged. South Africa has charged Israel with genocide in the world court, which, in turn, has ruled that Israel may be committing "plausible genocide."[45] Amnesty International has accused Israel of genocide in an official report.[46] In its unleashing of bombing, starvation, and displacement, Israel has become a pariah state. Furthermore, at the time of writing, many Israelis (Jewish, Arab, and Muslim) are moving their families to other countries in unprecedented numbers.[47] And yet, the state of Israel's response is the same: Bomb Gaza (and neighboring countries) and refute any criticism of the state of Israel as anti-Semitic bias that fails to acknowledge the horrors of October 7.

In the US, many Jewish communities seem cognizant of the consequences of deflecting criticism.[48] But I have been deeply disappointed by predominantly white, convert Buddhist institutions in the United States. I am not alone: South West Asian and North African Buddhists, as well as a number of prominent Jewish Buddhists, have also spoken out about the overwhelming silence from mainstream convert Buddhist organizations.[49] I have embraced Buddhism for its emphasis on clear-seeing (*vipassana*) and compassionate loving-kindness (*metta)*. I have been attuned to the multiple dimensions of fear that have wracked Jewish existence, having encountered it up close in my relationship with my godmother and her mother, who were Holocaust survivors. I have encountered it with Jewish friends and students. The fear operates on a cellular level. At the same time, it is clear that a number of different Buddhist lineages emphasize cultivating compassion for suffering, but they do not cultivate insight into the power dynamics at work.[50] Like other Buddhists who are struck by the silence of mainstream Buddhist organizations, I am coming up against the limits of compassion. I am observing that the practice of loving-kindness is only one wing of the bird. Clear seeing—blunt, unfiltered, nuanced—is necessary, too. And the practice of clear seeing can not only be relegated to individual feelings. To break through avoidance, to really take on suffering, we have to address power dynamics, including violent state power.

"Your silence will not protect you," Audre Lorde wrote. I have wrestled with how to speak out as a Buddhist practitioner. I can feel my fear and my protectiveness. I can feel my rage and my hatred. Buddhism has given me worldviews and practices for metabolizing the intensity of my feelings.

"But of course I am afraid," Audre Lorde said. Silence does not alleviate fear; if anything, it intensifies my rage and hatred.

"But we must speak, remembering, we were never meant to survive," Lorde stated.

The Karma of Right Action: Nuancing Experiences of Suffering, Metabolizing Rage

In speaking out, I have taken my cues from Baldwin and Lorde, and from scholars such as Rashid Khalidi, author of *The Hundred Years' War on Palestine*.[51] Khalidi advocates for conversations with Israelis and coexistence of Jews, Muslims, and Arabs in historical Mandatory Palestine. He is aware that his worldview is not accepted by many younger generations of activists.[52] But he points to his existence in the United States as an example: He, like many Jewish Israelis, lives on stolen, occupied land. The way forward is not expulsion, *of anyone*, but rather, coexistence.

I am committed to remaining engaged with worldviews that I do not understand. I am intrigued by the worldview of Jewish Israelis who feel that they cannot be safe unless they live in an ethnonationalist state that privileges Jewish identity. I have wanted to try and understand the emotional rationale that lies beneath it. The insistence on establishing a Jewish homeland on land that was already populated by people with their own ancestral connection is confusing to me. I am a Black American who has never, ever, been physically safe within the physical boundaries of the country in which I hold citizenship. I do not have the expectation that I will be safe. My lack of expectation is not due to a lack of trauma. My ancestors, too, have experienced annihilation, and more: the transatlantic trade of enslaved peoples, the auction block, physical brutality on penal farms and in chain gangs, Jim Crow segregation in all of its manifestations, mass incarceration. My people are experiencing the carceral violence of the US nation-state still. It is the reason that, on a gut level, my sympathies lie with Palestinians, who are routinely rounded up by police forces, governed under Israeli martial law, indefinitely incarcerated in detention centers, and made to survive without legal rights to their homes or adequate access to water. Their land is being stolen, violently. They are subjected to checkpoints, humiliated, and searched, constantly. Meanwhile, Jewish Israelis continue to commit atrocities without any accountability, with state support, with impunity.

I am far from the only Black activist to see parallels between Palestinian suffering and Black suffering. Suheir Hammad published *Born Palestinian, Born Black* in 1996.[53] Black Lives Matter activists in Ferguson relied on support from Palestinian activists when being tear-gassed during protests in 2015.[54] Scholars and journalists also make these connections.[55] Ta-Nehisi Coates, in his 2024 book *The Message,* compares twenty-first century Israeli society to the nineteenth-century and early twentieth-century Jim Crow South. He recognizes the limitations of his analogy, but he draws immediate and clear parallels between violent control of Palestinian bodies and land, and violent control of Black bodies, at every level of institution and interaction.[56] And he is not the only one. Prominent writers throughout the world, while expressing empathy for the historical suffering of European Jews whose families were exterminated in the Holocaust, hold the twenty-first-century state of Israel accountable for its atrocities. Artists, academics, government officials, UN officials, and clergy have expressed their horror at the occupation and ethnic cleansing of the West Bank and the genocide and ethnic cleansing in Gaza. I have continued to ask: Why can't white American Buddhists?

Like South West Asian and North African Buddhists, I do not want to disavow Buddhism because of my disappointment in predominantly white, convert Buddhist organizations. My Buddhist practice has saved my life; it has given me doctrines and rituals for healing. I claim it as a way forward. But I have long found an analysis of power lacking in American Buddhist communities. This fact is—in real time—coming to the forefront with the acknowledgment of sexual abuse in a number of different lineages.[57] And it is true with regards to other dynamics: authority concentrated in a single figure (a Zen priest or guru), and the ways in which finances are held and shared. This lack of focus on interrogating power dynamics operates on a larger level, too. Many Buddhist communities are unwilling to acknowledge systemic power, to name the violence of the state and how it operates disproportionately on certain bodies and identities: dark-skinned, female, transgender, undocumented. There is an omission with regard to US-sponsored military power and conquest. White American Buddhists have sought to create compassionate refuge without a corresponding commitment to seeing mundane reality clearly. What is called clear seeing instead often functions as myopia.

This strikes me as avoidant at the very least, a perpetuation of racism in its most extreme form. I hear Baldwin's indictment of white evasion when I read the statements put out by predominantly white, convert Buddhist organizations.[58] What is Buddhism if not the cultivation of muscles to encounter suffering, to behold it, nuance it, feel through it, and develop a broad and deep capacity for compassionate action?[59] In my understanding, Buddhism calls me forth to address widespread harm and trauma, not to avoid the nuances of power by evoking terms like "enlightenment."

I claim the Buddhist tradition precisely because it has provided doctrines and practices to confront suffering—on multiple dimensions—and stay with it, not avoid it. In the same vein, I am encountering the distinct suffering of Palestinians experiencing occupation, ethnic cleansing, and genocide. I am committed to Palestinian liberation in the same way that I am committed to Black liberation. It is incumbent upon me to build the muscles to work for Palestinian liberation, despite my exhaustion, despite my fear. One way I have committed to the Karma of Right Action is to take seriously the charge of anti-Semitism and to seek to understand the nuances of it. I have quickly learned that this could take a lifetime. Distinct worldviews and complicated histories underly the term "anti-Semitism" and various definitions of it offered by Jewish political organizations. Many American Jews also indict the right-wing Israeli government for politicizing the term and diluting the very real experiences of discrimination and hatred of Jews erupting around the world.

In light of the enormous literature by Jewish intellectuals and pundits—many of whom critique the state of Israel and many of whom see Israel as central to their identity—the Karma of Right Action, for me personally, is to attempt to read as many varied perspectives as possible. It is incumbent upon me not to dismiss Jewish suffering, even if it is articulated in ways that I find offensive, even reprehensible. It is my work to take it all in and, when I find myself in a state of rage and hatred, to sit with my aversion rather than react out of it. I continue to remember Baldwin's words: "To be a Negro in this country and to be relatively conscious is to be in a state of rage almost all of the time."[60] It is incumbent upon me to cultivate the muscles to sit with horror and not look away or write off the people committing the atrocities.

I expend tremendous emotional labor attempting to see clearly and to work through my rage, confusion, and fear. I also come up against my limitations; I have found that I cannot maintain close relationships with Jewish members of my community who say extremely offensive things to me. I can listen and ask questions, but I am aware of when I do not feel safe. It is a both-and: I am sensitive to anti-Semitism and do not want to perpetuate it. At the same time, I feel the intensity of racism articulated by many pro-Israel Jews who dismiss Palestinian suffering. I am taking time to hold it all together: standing up for Palestinians but not perpetuating Jewish suffering as a result of ignorance and aversion. This, for me, is the Karma of Right Action.

It is important to speak out against atrocity with nuance. As a self-identified Buddhist, I have taken two stands publicly. I state that I do not support any ethnonationalist states. With regards to Israel, I state that Palestinians deserve full civil, political, and social rights in the region known as "from the river to the sea." This is hardly a radical stance; younger Jews and American Jewish scholars have been saying this for decades, since the occupation began in 1967.[61] The second stance that I have taken, actively, is to align my commitments to Palestinian liberation to my commitments to the Black Freedom movement in the US and South Africa. I state that justice and peace for all peoples, Palestinians and Jews alike, cannot take place within a carceral system, and that I stand against the carceral policies of any nation-state that actively detains, imprisons, and separates large swaths of its population. This includes Israel.[62]

This, for me, is the Karma of Right Action. It begins with acknowledging *specific* forms of suffering. It confronts and seeks to dismantle state violence. It is protective. I steep myself in Palestinian voices. And I intentionally internalize myriad Jewish perspectives and take seriously Jewish suffering. The Karma of Right Thought, Words, and Action means fostering compassion and honoring rage, and cultivating the muscles to hold it all.

"We must speak, remembering, we were never meant to survive," Audre Lorde wrote.

To speak on behalf of people assaulted by state violence—or to self-silence—is our karma.

PRACTICE
Allying with Fire

The following is a practice from Lama Rod Owens's 2024 book *The New Saints (used with permission).*[63] This is one way that I have encountered for metabolizing collective grief and rage. I engaged in a similar practice with a group of spiritually oriented activists who are committed to supporting Palestinians in Gaza and the West Bank. Turning toward the fire, feeling its warmth on a very cold night, I acknowledged how the elements change and shift. I witnessed the truth of impermanence. We offered sacred items to fuel the flames. Even with the onslaught of tremendous violence against Palestinians in Gaza and the West Bank, watching the fire, I witnessed the possibility of alchemy and transformation.

CEREMONY FROM LAMA ROD OWENS

The fire prayer ceremony is one of my favorite ceremonies and one of the most powerful ceremonies I perform. My practice of the fire prayer ceremony is based on ancient Indian Vedic ceremonies and Tibetan fire ceremonies. I have adapted these influences to create a ceremony that is innovative and fluid. I never do a ceremony the same way twice because I am interested in allowing the ceremony to adjust to my needs at the moment.

The fire prayer ceremony has two purposes in the New Saints' tradition. First, it is a way to connect and ally with the fire element and the deities connected to fire. "Allyship" means that we are open to the consciousness of fire and its role in maintaining the spiritual ecology, and from that openness, we can learn how it is helping us get free.

Second, we practice a fire ceremony to transmute or change substances from one thing to another. In this case, substances like food or herbs are offered to the fire. As the fire is burning the food, the essential energy of the substance is released from its material form, and our prayers can then direct that energy toward helping ourselves and other beings.

HOLDING A FIRE CEREMONY

A fire ceremony can be done with a large outdoor fire or a burning stick of incense or anything in between. The important elements of the practice are fire, substances that can be burned, and prayers. Here I offer general instructions for a larger ceremony offered outside.

First, gather up the items that you would like to offer. If you're unsure, you can make a simple offering of a small bowl of grains, candy, and incense. Then set up a fire that is manageable for you, like a small campfire, and light it.

Second, when the fire is going, bless the fire by dipping a finger into a cup of water and flicking water on the fire three times. This gesture acknowledges that the fire is now being used to benefit beings. The gesture also helps to invite the water element into the ceremony, which encourages the fluidity and movement of the energy you will begin releasing.

Third, imagine that all the fire in the universe begins to collect in your third chakra, the energy center located in your solar plexus, around your navel, which holds a lot of fire energy already. As you collect and hold the fire, recite the following prayer:

> The heat of my body is the heat that drives the universe. Precious fire, you change and transform, transmute and demolish, light and warm, release and relax. My heat is the fire of lava erupting from the earth's core to forest fires, the light of stars, the sun, all the way back to the warmth in my gut. My anger is fire raging, springing from my broken heart and ready to ignite the world in flames. When I listen to you, I am listening to the heartbeat of life and death itself, the constant burning away and emerging of what needs to emerge. I am the phoenix rising from the ashes of my own heartbreak. I pray to the precious

fire element and all the deities connected to it to support this ceremony as I make offerings and pray for the benefit of all beings.

Now, imagine releasing the fire collected in your third chakra into the fire itself. Imagine that the fire is now ready for the ceremony.

Fourth, invite your ancestors and all benevolent beings, including deities, to join the space around you so that they can enjoy these offerings as well.

Fifth, hold the offering bowl and reflect on why you are making the offering and who or what you hope it benefits.

Sixth, offer the material into the fire. As the material begins to burn, imagine that its essential energy is being released into the world. Begin offering prayers as you imagine this energy being directed into the situations you are praying for. You can even imagine that the smoke from the fire permeates the land you are on, blessing all beings with what they need to be well and experience liberation.

Finally, when you feel complete, thank the fire for its kindness and all the beings for supporting the ceremony. To complete the ceremony, imagine that all beings are experiencing liberation from this ceremony and rest in the joy that may arise from that thought.

Pain That Saves Your Life

The Blessed One said, "When touched with a feeling of pain, the uninstructed run-of-the-mill person sorrows, grieves, & laments, beats his breast, becomes distraught. So he feels two pains, physical & mental. Just as if they were to shoot a man with an arrow and, right afterward, were to shoot him with another one, so that he would feel the pains of two arrows; in the same way, when touched with a feeling of pain, the uninstructed run-of-the-mill person sorrows, grieves, & laments, beats his breast, becomes distraught. So he feels two pains, physical & mental."

—SALLATHA SUTTA

James Baldwin, Audre Lorde, and the Buddha helped me discern a way forward as I sought to metabolize my rage and grief. This was true politically, and it was true in the most personal ways. I looked to them as luminaries who had found ways to work effectively with suffering. Baldwin and Lorde had suffered the pain of oppression due to their dark skin and sexuality; they had suffered the pain of being hated within their own families. These were first-arrow pains: harm directed at them. Yet rather than succumb to rage and anxiety, rather than repress or project their pain onto others, they turned toward it and sought to know it intimately.

They sought to understand their pain even at an early age. Lorde wrote often of the fact that she did not speak until she was four. She was also legally blind. She encountered the world around her through blurry images. She listened deeply as she observed. When she began to speak, she articulated herself in poems. Feeling, fragments of images, and close observation guided her. She learned to validate her own particular experience of her environment.

Her stories of early childhood resonated with me; so, too, did Baldwin's. I could identify with their hunger for protection and care within families in which they were disparaged. They sought refuge from the hostile environment of New York City. Yet the aggression also took place within their own families.

I, too, was born into a large, unfriendly city—Chicago—defenseless against forces of contempt, compelled to navigate animosity on my own. Like Baldwin and Lorde, I encountered hostility and rejection within my family: in my case, from my mother's parents.

My grandparents were descendants of Eastern European immigrants who sought to "become white," as Baldwin would say.[1] They were desperate for what Baldwin called "The Price of the Ticket"[2]—white identity at the expense of everything else. They made it clear that my dark skin stood in the way of their social progress.

Their response to my birth was to deny my existence. This was obvious to me at a very early age. One of my first recollections is staring at the bulletin board in my grandparents' kitchen, looking at the school photos of my white cousins, tacked in a tidy row. I was nowhere to be found. Over the years, the range of photos became more extensive. My white cousins, one older and one younger, grew and assumed my grandparents' features. I, too, looked like them: I possessed the same full cheeks, curved forehead, baggy eyes. And still, I was not included. I was the dark one, born "illegitimate," out of wedlock. I was a reminder of secrets, of shame.

My grandparents' denial of me, their Black granddaughter, appeared solid, immovable. Like stone. I circled around it throughout my adolescence, testing their willingness to acknowledge their racism, seeking clarity about *why* they rejected me. Their hostility manifested as hatred, and it took hold of my nervous system. Even when I did not see them, I was aware of their judgment. I performed, I think, to gain their approval. Later, when I was eighteen, I framed a photo of us that was taken at my high school graduation. My grandparents are standing on either side of me, smiling. I too am grinning widely, my hair long and curly, my hands holding my diploma. During the next family gathering, I looked for the photo. Eventually I found it, hidden in the family room, tucked away in a space that visitors did not enter.

Hidden away. Unacknowledged. Unwanted. There is suffering in life, the Buddha said, speaking of the Four Noble Truths and the Noble Eightfold Path. There is suffering that arises from causes and conditions. Pain lands on us, but it's what we do with it that matters. We can work skillfully with our pain and not turn it into suffering.

I absorbed this message. But I was still suspicious. It was coming from a man who was born a prince, two thousand six hundred years prior to my birth. *There is suffering in life.* I needed translators. I found them in James Baldwin and Audre Lorde.

"A Wilderness of Smashed Plate Glass"

The year James Baldwin turned nineteen, his stepfather died. It had been a difficult relationship, one which Baldwin describes in his evocative essay "Notes of a Native Son" and in his first novel, *Go Tell It on the Mountain.* His stepfather had been cruel. Baldwin resisted the abuse, first by turning toward books and plays, and then, in his adolescence, the church. He eventually left the church, turned off by myths he could not believe in and the hypocrisy that he observed. He became once again absorbed by books and plays. As he came of age, Baldwin observed the steady decay of his stepfather's mind into terror and madness. Eventually, he left home and stayed with friends in Greenwich Village. He returned to Harlem for his stepfather's funeral, making his way through an environment he called "a wilderness of smashed plate glass."[3]

Baldwin was still figuring out who he was and making sense of the world around him when he attended his stepfather's funeral. It was much later that he began to feel empathy for a man who had belittled and rejected him. Baldwin came to see his stepfather as a sensitive Southern patriarch who could not, despite his hardest efforts, adequately feed his children in the North. He had migrated from the brutalities of Jim Crow to Harlem, an environment that relegated Black people to degrading positions of inferiority. Black people could only live in run-down, rat-infested apartments. They were only allowed to work menial, low-paying jobs. Northern white authorities—welfare caseworkers, police officers, bosses—still treated Black people with contempt and violence. The mean slums of the North were no better than the vicious towns of the South.

His stepfather, Baldwin realized, had operated from a perpetual bedrock of fear. He had been a proud, powerful man, but he had also been afraid. White people could not be trusted; the world around him could never be safe. His stepfather had constantly reacted to daily humiliations, to violence. Their family was always on the verge of eviction, on the edge of starvation, weathering the instability that comes with being held on the bottom rung of the social ladder. They were perpetually dismissed and ignored. In this atmosphere of hostility and uncertainty, Baldwin's stepfather had not been able to connect to his own inner life or to the lives of his children.

When Baldwin reflected upon and acknowledged his stepfather's suffering, he was able to encounter his own.

Suffering in the Early Buddhist Tradition

In the early Buddhist tradition, the Pali word *dukkha* is translated as "suffering," or sometimes "the painful." In Buddhism, the term "dukkha" encompasses numerous aspects of suffering: physical pain, mental afflictions, and emotional devastation.

I spent years parsing these dimensions of dukkha. I appreciated a tradition that nuanced the varied ways in which suffering could show up. I was particularly aware of the intensity of my anxiety: a rapid heartbeat if I heard an odd noise, or if I said the wrong thing. I would often disassociate when I felt overwhelmed by fear. When I encountered the *Sallatha Sutta*, two feelings arose: validation and regret. On the one hand, my anxiety was justified—arrows can pierce when they land on us from out of the blue, including from our own families. And yet, I became aware that I was often suffering as a result of inflicting pain upon myself. This was something over which I had agency.

The *Sallatha Sutta* tells a story about the two dimensions of dukkha. In its extended version, it conveys the narrative of a man who was unexpectedly shot with an arrow. Shortly after being shot, he was abandoned by the people around him. The bleeding man stumbled about, alone and afraid. He suffered excruciating physical pain from the arrow protruding from his arm. He began to worry. He was by himself. How could he seek help? He worried that he would die. If he collapsed, would animals tear his flesh to pieces and eat him? Would his family find out? The man spun deeper and deeper into a whirlwind of anxiety.

The *Sallatha Sutta*—known as the "Tale of Two Arrows"—teaches that there is a first arrow—an uncontrollable experience, a set of conditions—that results in pain or harm. The second arrow is less obvious but no less potent. It refers to the thoughts and mental anxieties that escalate suffering.

Baldwin, like the *Sallatha Sutta*, tells us that we can't always control the first arrow. We live in environments that often take us down because they are unrelentingly brutal. He saw this with his stepfather, with the young people in Harlem with whom he came of age. He reflected upon the narratives that Black people absorbed as though they were true. Like my experience of my white grandparents, whose shame I internalized, Baldwin noticed that he and his stepfather—that all Black people—were deemed inferior in the eyes of white people. Absorbing these messages, like breathing air, shapes us and can drive us to madness if we do not develop perspectives and practices to confront and uproot them.

In early Buddhism, the practice of confronting suffering effectively is called *upaya*. This Pali term is translated as "skillful means." It conveys that there are skillful ways in which to work with suffering, and that it is unskillful to try to avoid it.

Seeing Beauty in That Which Is Considered Polluted

The first step to working with suffering is to look at it. In my own life, this meant noticing my feelings of validation and regret. It was important to acknowledge the pain, to see that it came from somewhere, to name the particular aspects of it. I suffered from exposure to my grandparents' harmful behavior, from a lack of protection. These conditions were important to name. But I had, in turn, adapted to that toxicity in ways that did not serve me. I was constantly performing, seeking validation and approval. My Buddhist practice taught me that if I did not learn skillful ways to respond to hatred and alienation, I would continue to respond unconsciously to the harmful arrow of my grandparents' hatred. I would continue to harm myself.

I looked to Baldwin as a model. He had confronted his pain and had recognized the ways in which he had absorbed toxic messages. He saw that he continued to move in the world as though those narratives were true. He had internalized the message that he was ugly, unworthy of excellence. In learning to see beauty in ugliness, he developed a way of taking on his stepfather's mockery. Baldwin would sometimes tell the story of how once, when he was a teenager, he and his mentor, Beauford Delaney, were out walking on the Lower East Side. At one point, Delaney pointed to a patch of oil in the gutter and told Baldwin to "look" and "look again." Baldwin noticed how the swirling liquid reflected the clouds above in a starkly evocative way. It was a lesson that stayed with Baldwin: There was beauty in that which was considered polluted, if we could learn to closely observe it.[4]

These were important lessons for Baldwin; these were important lessons for me, too. I was told that as a result of the color of my skin, I was unworthy of love. To compensate, I was constantly serving and performing. It was only when I stopped to ask about the depth of my suffering and the conditions that lay beneath it that I developed the skillful means—the upaya—to see beauty where my grandparents saw defilement.

This was the beginning of my Buddhist practice. When I first learned meditation, I was instructed to observe and count my breath. In so doing, I was told, I would learn to still my mind and cultivate awareness of the body. This practice was fruitful in my first year. I learned how to simply see what was in my mind; I learned how to identify the nuances of others' behaviors that unconsciously fueled so many of my thoughts and actions.

This was the first step to liberation: learning how to see. Awareness and healing require strategies. Baldwin had inspired me; Buddhism offered me the tools to learn how to realize the insights that Baldwin cultivated in himself.

Bearing the Intimacy of Scrutiny

Baldwin articulated the nuances of his suffering: He named what it was like to be Black and impoverished in America; how queer-identified persons were shunned and marginalized. So, too, did Audre Lorde. In her essays, journal entries, and interviews, Audre Lorde expressed her capacity to turn toward different dimensions of suffering and to know these layers intimately. Pain is bearable, Lorde said. But in order to hold it, to move through it, we need the capacity to stay with it, to behold it as valuable. Developing the capacity to stay with pain requires the intention to sit with oneself. This is hard, and necessary. It is the foundation of change. Lorde wrote:

> The quality of light by which we scrutinize our lives has direct bearing upon the product which we live, and upon the changes we hope to bring about through those lives. It is within this light that we form those ideas by which we pursue our magic and make it realized. . . . As we learn to bear the intimacy of scrutiny and to flourish within it, as we learn to use the products of that scrutiny for power within our living, those fears which rule our lives and form our silences begin to lose their control over us.[5]

Lorde is not saying that we suffer *because* we scrutinize; instead, the practice of self-scrutiny is what occurs in place of the second arrow. It brings an intensity of awareness to the source of pain, and in concentrating attention on our pain—and the whole of our lives—we encounter inner stability, unshakable authority. The early Buddhist suttas lift up the practice of cultivating awareness of old age, sickness, and death—the impermanence of our lives—as a practice of liberation from suffering. Lorde, too, was pointing to scrutinizing our inner lives as a practice of freedom.

Moreover, ignoring pain creates more pain. This is the second arrow. The first arrow harms us. This is the pain that is part of living. It is when we try to avoid the pain it causes that we bring upon ourselves the suffering of the second arrow. Acknowledging pain is an initial step to freeing ourselves from it.

I could acknowledge the pain. It was "bearing the intimacy of scrutiny" that was harder. When I turned toward my experience of being excluded from my mother's family, I could feel how tightly I was wound. It was like a knot of hard steel had become lodged in my chest. It took all of my energy to breathe through it. Two years into my meditation practice, when I learned about loving-kindness practice and how to "take refuge" in the Buddha, the Dharma, and the Sangha, I was able to create some softness around the pain. I was able to bear the intimacy of scrutiny without flinching. For many years thereafter, my Buddhist practice was just that: bearing. There were specific instructions on how to meditate: how to fold my hands, hold my back upright, count my breaths, cultivate compassion. But most importantly, I learned how to stay with everything that arose. Sometimes the thoughts were so powerful that I feared being swept away. But I tried to breathe through them. To bear them.

And Audre Lorde was right. My fear loosened over time. My self-silencing was less pronounced. I started to be more relaxed, more able to handle the waves that came my way. I felt safer in my own body. Able to flourish. I could conceive of my own power.

Trust Your Experience

Bearing scrutiny rests on trust. Baldwin, like Lorde, saw the second arrow of suffering, and wanted something different for himself: another way of being, an ability to be vulnerable with others, a capacity to trust himself and his environment. He yearned to live with a depth of intimacy that could interface with fear, and at the same time, not be ruled by fear. He desired to turn toward the anguish that arose from fear and to know that anguish fully.

Baldwin observed the devastation of the first arrow: the conditions of Harlem, the narratives of inferiority. He felt the devastation in himself. He was attuned to the swiftness with which he could fall into a vortex of despair or rage. And yet, he said, we can choose our responses to everything that happens to us. We can cultivate new ways of encountering the suffering that is inevitable. The first arrow of poverty, violence, and narratives of Black inferiority inflicts pain. We don't have to suffer the second arrow.

Baldwin conveyed this message directly in a letter to his nephew in *The Fire Next Time*, a book of essays he published in 1962. He wrote about his stepfather—his nephew's grandfather—as a man who "really believed what white people said about him."[6] Baldwin's stepfather had been "certainly the most bitter man I have ever met. . . . He claimed to be proud of his blackness, but it had also been the cause of much humiliation and had fixed bleak boundaries to his life."[7]

Baldwin told his nephew: "You can only be destroyed by believing that you really are what the white world calls a *nigger*. I tell you this because I love you, and please don't you ever forget it."[8]

Baldwin acknowledged the first arrow of vicious racism. And in so doing, he refused the second arrow of internalizing inferiority. He wrote to his nephew:

> You were born where you were born and faced the future that you faced because you were black and *for no other reason*. The limits of your ambition were, thus, expected to be set forever. You were born into a society which spelled out with brutal clarity, and in as many ways as possible, that you were a worthless human being. You were not expected to aspire to excellence: you were expected to make peace with mediocrity.[9]

Baldwin anticipated that white people would dismiss his experience and point to ways in which Black people had "made progress" by adopting white values. But Baldwin refused to submerge his voice. He attuned instead to the violence of his upbringing and the injustices that Black people are expected to accept as normal. He refused the definitions, the gaslighting, of the white world. He recalled the ways in which he had been made to feel inferior in his own home—called "ugly" and disparaged intellectually. He instructed his nephew: "Take no one's word for anything including mine—but trust your experience."[10]

I internalized these words as a set of directions. Baldwin was saying, this is what we've been handed, this is the landscape we are forced to navigate. Uphill, downhill, rocky, flat. Whatever comes our way, we can walk through it. And continue. If we can trust ourselves, one foot forward at a time. The affirmation that came with looking at my suffering was that way forward. In my Buddhist tradition, I was trained to do this. Over and over again.

Confronting suffering, Baldwin said, is a practice, a path. "Know whence you came," he instructed his nephew. He was telling his nephew to encounter and feel *everything*, to give oxygen to the rage and sorrow, the anxieties, the feelings of helplessness, even sensual energy—to let it all breathe. In so doing, he said, human beings achieve agency, power, the capacity to change our conditions, decolonize our minds, rather than "be controlled by a fear of what life can bring."[11] The capacity to acknowledge the devastating conditions around us and how we have internalized them makes us human, empathic, worthy of life.

See How Much of This Pain I Can Use

Audre Lorde, too, illuminated this message. We suffer, and the devastation that lands on us can be used for learning and growth. In a 1982 interview, Lorde said, "It's one thing to talk about feeling. It's another to feel. Yes, love is often pain. But I think what is really necessary is to see how much of this pain I can use, how much of this truth I can see and still live unblinded."[12]

Pain is inevitable. But it can be used for growth, for change. We can relate to our suffering skillfully.

Confronting fear, and other forms of suffering, requires a kind of muscle, stamina. But once we cultivate the capacity to confront pain, Lorde said, pain and suffering can be acknowledged as useful, generative.

In illuminating suffering as a teacher, Lorde recounted an experience of a window falling on her arm. She called for help, but it was seven minutes before someone found her. Lorde reflected:

> It was crucial, that seven minutes. In it I lived the whole history of pain from start to finish. . . . The choice was immediate: to die, or to bear the pain. And what does bearing mean? It means

changing, or going through. It is not death. It is an experience encapsulated. It could stop. It could be ended. By chewing off my arm, for example. But this was not possible for me. So the pain is transformed. The intensity changes. It has to stop or it has to change. This was a physical knowledge that I had not had before, that pain has a mutability. This is very, very important, and that is just as true about emotional pain: it will change or stop.[13]

Rather than collapsing from the first arrow—the physical pain of the falling window—Lorde chose to use the pain in the process of gaining perspective. Everything that emerges or lands, welcome or not, can be used for growth and change. Lorde continued:

I felt at that point that there was nothing I could not do, nothing that I could not deal with, because pain will always either change or stop. Always . . . The confidence that it will change is what makes *bearing* possible. So pain is fluid. It is only when you conceive of it as something static that it is unbearable.[14]

Liberation from suffering rests on awareness and *practice* of what is required for growth. It involves rooting out internalized oppression as well as recognizing how oppressed persons have been divided against each other. We have been taught to fear pain and expressions of anger. And yet. Liberation requires confronting pain. Diving into suffering—rather than avoiding it (the second arrow)—cultivates fearlessness. This fearlessness can be practiced and cultivated if pain can be acknowledged as useful.

I saw this in my own life as my Buddhist practice deepened. In my first year of practice, I had learned how to see the nuances of my suffering. Over time, I had started to develop skillful ways of meeting my anxiety and grief. I learned to be nonreactive, to observe and behold the feelings that arose before communicating with other people. Perhaps most importantly, I stopped blaming other people for my suffering. Yes, my grandparents had harmed me in deeply consequential ways. They had made clear that they wished I had not been born.

They made known their shame of my appearance. But as I internalized Audre Lorde's message of useful pain through my Buddhist practice, I began to see my grandparents' harm as an arrow of pain that I could metabolize, as a force from which I could learn to see more clearly. My grandparents' hatred gave me a window into the suffering of Palestinians, of all people who are unwanted or considered disposable. Their hatred, rather than submerging me, was a means to develop insight and compassion.

Turning toward pain is inseparable from gaining strength, and ultimately, interior and political freedom. Lorde named growth that comes from confronting pain as a survival skill particularly honed by Black people. She wrote: "One of the most basic Black survival skills is the ability to change, to metabolize experience, good or ill, into something that is useful, lasting, effective."[15] As Lorde described the specific oppressions encountered by Black people, she consistently emphasized the importance of working effectively with painful emotions.

In her essay "Learning from the Sixties," she noted that we must recognize the harmful narratives that we have internalized.

> If our history has taught us anything, it is that action for change directed only against the external conditions of our oppressions is not enough. In order to be whole, we must recognize the despair oppression plants within each of us—that thin, persistent voice that says our efforts are useless, it will never change, so why bother, accept it. And we must fight that inserted piece of self-destruction that lives and flourishes like a poison inside of us, unexamined until it makes us turn upon ourselves in each other. But we can put our finger down upon that loathing buried deep within each one of us and see who it encourages us to despise, and we can lessen its potency by the knowledge of our real connectedness, arcing across our differences.[16]

The self-scrutiny that Lorde pointed to again and again rests upon training the mind to see clearly the origins of suffering and how we act out our suffering. Allowing herself to *feel*, rather than repress, allowing herself to *acknowledge*, rather than deny, evolved her power. Allowing space to feel helps us take back the weapons from enemies' hands and stop directing arrows toward those closest to us as we grapple with the second arrow of fear. "To search for power within myself means I must be willing to move through being afraid to whatever lies beyond. If I look at my most vulnerable places and acknowledge the pain I have felt, I can remove the source of that pain from my enemies' arsenals," Lorde wrote.[17]

That was true for me as well. In my Buddhist practice, I had come up against an emotional pain so searing that it was worse than breaking a bone. If I could tolerate such emotional anguish, a gun pointed at me was minimal. That was, at root, the practice of meditation. Confronting pain directly, willingly. A practice of fearlessness.

Lorde's message is clear: We must meet our pain. But, like the *Sallatha Sutta*, she made a distinction between pain and suffering. Pain—the first arrow—is an experience beyond our control. Pain can be used for growth. Suffering is different from pain; it is a second arrow that we aim at ourselves and those closest to us, unnecessarily, thereby wasting the insights that can be gained from facing pain. While experiencing past pain can feel like hurling oneself against a concrete wall, Lorde reflected, confronting it is necessary for survival:

> There is a distinction I am beginning to make in my living between *pain* and *suffering*. Pain is an event, an experience that must be recognized, named, and then used in some way in order for the experience to change, to be transformed into something else, strength or knowledge or action.
>
> Suffering, on the other hand, is the nightmare of reliving unscrutinized and unmetabolized pain. When I live through pain without recognizing it, self-consciously, I rob myself of the power that can come from *using* that pain, the power to fuel some movement beyond it. I condemn myself to reliving that pain over and over and over whenever something close triggers it. And that is suffering, a seemingly inescapable cycle.[18]

Metabolizing pain—refusing the second arrow of unscrutinized suffering and honoring all aspects of our emotional life—fuels our capacity for power.

Power

Lorde pointed to the concept of "power" as the internal force that propels us to "bear" suffering, and in so doing, to gain control over our lives. Bearing suffering does not relegate us to the position of a doormat; on the contrary, it requires strength that extends to every other aspect of daily life. When we develop the capacity to bear suffering, we cultivate interior strength. We can face damaging narratives of the dominant culture and how we have internalized them; we can embrace new ways of being. In bearing suffering, the grip of fear that clutches our minds lessens and falls away. Scrutinizing ourselves and cultivating fearlessness shift our relationships to our own inner lives and each other.

Over and over again, Lorde redefined power as a force that leads to fearlessness, to confrontation with violent intimidation and authority. When encountering the internalized voices that women have been taught to fear, we become capable of defining power on our own terms. This power to redefine ourselves, Lorde said, is different from white, patriarchal ideas of power. The patriarchal model uplifts rational thinking. It privileges analysis and external structures. Lorde contested this definition of power by uplifting the importance of honoring feeling, including the experience of suffering. Power, for Lorde, does not revolve around intellectual presumptions; it arises from creative, emotional expressions. It arises from intuitive knowledge. Here Lorde pointed to the power of honoring our interior lives:

Within these deep places, each one of us holds an incredible reserve of creativity and power, of unexamined and unrecorded emotion and feeling. The woman's place of power within each of us is neither white nor surface; it is dark, it is ancient, and it is deep. When we view living in the European mode only as a problem to be solved, we rely solely upon our ideas to make us free, for these were what the white fathers told us were precious. But as we come more into touch with our own ancient, non-European consciousness of living as a situation to be experienced and interacted with, we learn more and more to cherish our feelings, and to respect those hidden sources of our power from where true knowledge and, therefore, lasting action comes.[19]

Lorde connected creativity and power with the examined life, with self-scrutiny. There is power in the ability to look inward and take account of our feelings and the conditions into which we are born. It is a practice that can be done instead of being victimized by the second arrow. It is a practice of taking refuge.

I resonated with Audre Lorde's definition of power as I developed my Buddhist practice over time. It was difficult to think of myself as a powerful person, but as I cultivated inner stability, I found myself willing to challenge ideas that I was expected to accept. I began to be less afraid of rejection. I saw this as I confronted the internalized messages from my grandparents.

Lorde's emphasis on honoring suffering—on turning toward feelings, regardless of how excruciating or vile they might seem—leads to a capacity to acknowledge harm without shutting down. In her view, our embrace—rather than repression—of difficult emotions fosters a powerful capacity for openness. Lorde wrote:

As they become known to and accepted by us, our feelings and the honest exploration of them become sanctuaries and spawning grounds for the most radical and daring of ideas. They become a safe-house for that difference so necessary to change and the conceptualization of any meaningful action. . . . *We can train ourselves* to respect our feelings and to transpose them into a language so they can be shared.[20]

I resonated with Lorde's term "safe-house." This language suggested refuge. In embracing Buddhist practice, I had learned how to take refuge, to cultivate an interior security so that all feelings, regardless of how intense they are, would have a place to land and be known.

But cultivating refuge did not come easily. Developing such interior security required discipline. Lorde saw that cultivating a "safe-house" required training and affirmed that we, as humans who experience the first arrow of pain, have to do the hard work of evolving. In order to be internally secure and able to resist internalizing harmful messages, we have to train our minds. This is how we build the capacity to honor differences among ourselves.

In my own Buddhist practice, this is daily work. It requires steadiness that slowly heals wounds over time. My grandparents had not invited self-scrutiny in themselves; they were solely concerned with blaming others for their shortcomings. And they had been cruel. I did not want to be like them; I sought the security that arises from self-scrutiny for myself. And it required the mental training described by Lorde.

In speaking of training the mind and heart, Lorde mirrors the early Buddhist suttas. Training the mind to see clearly involves staying with one's feelings and allowing them to be articulated in language and images, rather than repressing them out of fear. Pain, Lorde mused, surfaces in dreams. And dreams, she believed, point the way to freedom. Honoring feelings, including pain, ultimately fosters the experience of liberation for all people who have been oppressed.

What arose in my dreams? I pondered this as I read Lorde's essays. I dreamed of possessing the capacity and time to revel in beauty. I dreamed of safety, connection, of feeling like I was enough. I dreamed of moving from inner stability, no matter how strong the winds that blew my way.

Unshakable Authority

Possessing inner stability, a depth of presence, and unshakable authority was a message threaded throughout Baldwin's essays and interviews over several decades. Like Audre Lorde, Baldwin wrote of the authority that arises from confronting suffering. There are those who *can* suffer, Baldwin said, and those who cannot. The capacity to suffer requires an intimacy with one's own life. It requires skill.

In *The Fire Next Time*, Baldwin wrote:

> People who cannot suffer can never grow up, can never discover who they are. That man who is forced each day to snatch his manhood, his identity, out of the fire of human cruelty that rages to destroy it knows . . . something about himself and human life that no school on earth—and indeed, no church—can teach. He achieves his own authority, and that is unshakable. This is because, in order to save his own life, he is forced to look beneath appearances, to take nothing for granted, to hear the meaning behind the words. If one is continually surviving the worst that life can bring, one eventually ceases to be controlled by a fear of what life can bring; whatever it brings must be borne.[21]

Baldwin was optimistic even in the face of great anguish. I absorbed from him the message that if we develop the capacity to suffer, we achieve an inner foundation. We achieve power. We cease to be controlled by "a fear of what life can bring." That fearlessness and capacity to confront suffering, Baldwin insisted, are the bedrock for challenging all forms of oppression: the first arrow conditions of hatred and the second arrow states of mind that can be trained and emancipated. I gravitated toward Baldwin's language of "unshakable authority." I carried the words around with me on slips of paper. I put them on my office wall. I quoted them, time and again, to my students. I internalized the promise that even as pain comes at us, it need not be the last word. We can train our minds to meet the pain skillfully; we can use it for growth. Ultimately, we will embody unshakable authority.

PRACTICE
Mindfulness of the Body and Breath

The following meditation instruction on mindfulness of the body and breath has been a daily practice for me for more than two decades. I am inspired by my friend Valerie Mason-John (Vimalasara), a teacher in the Triratna Buddhist lineage. I am also influenced by movement instructions from Gabrielle Roth, who designed 5Rhythms body practices.[22]

Body practices offer a foundation for paying attention to my body and creating a sense of refuge. By paying attention to what my body is feeling and how my breath is entering and leaving my body, I shift from a highly intellectual mode of being—including anxious second-arrow thoughts—to a more attuned way of being. I put my attention to the natural rhythms of my body, becoming more aware of how my body breathes by itself. I become both more aware of my thoughts and less attached to them. I do not judge anything that comes to mind; I only focus on creating awareness and attunement. These practices create a deep sense of inner relaxation and ease for me.

BODY SCAN PRACTICE

This can be done while dancing, sitting, or lying down. Try to spend at least one minute moving each body part described below:

1. Pay attention to your head and neck. Notice the angle at which you are holding your head, if you are bent forward or tilted, and if you are feeling tension or tightness. Breathe in, breathe out.

2. Pay attention to your shoulders. Notice if you feel tightness in your trapezoids and your shoulder blades. You may want to move or massage your shoulders while you relax. Breathe in, breathe out.

3. Attune to your elbows. While you are dancing, sitting, or lying down, move your elbows and notice the feelings in your arms, whether there is soreness and strength, and any tiredness or stiffness. Breathe in, breathe out.

4. Move your hands. You may squeeze them open and shut, or flap them like wings. Notice the many bones and ligaments that make up your hands. Breathe in, breathe out.

5. Move your spine. If you are standing up and dancing, or sitting on your cushion, you may want to bend forward and backward, giving a deep stretch to the part of your body that holds you upright. Breathe in, breathe out.

6. Attune to your hips. You may want to sway side to side, noticing the stretch of your muscles and the feeling that arises in your back. Breathe in, breathe out.

7. Move your knees. Attune to any stiffness or achiness that may arise, any places that would benefit from deep stretching. Breathe in, breathe out.

8. Pay attention to your feet. You may want to simply bend them or you may want to lift them high. Breathe in, breathe out.

Sun in a Sunless Place

There are these five facts that one should reflect on often, whether one is . . . lay or ordained. Which five?

> *"I am subject to aging, have not gone beyond aging." This is the first fact that one should reflect on often, whether one is . . . lay or ordained.*
>
> *"I am subject to illness, have not gone beyond illness. . . ."*
>
> *"I am subject to death, have not gone beyond death. . . ."*
>
> *"I will grow different, separate from all that is dear and appealing to me. . . ."*
>
> *"I am the owner of my actions, heir to my actions, born of my actions, related through my actions, and have my actions as my arbitrator. Whatever I do, for good or for evil, to that will I fall heir. . . ."*

These are the five facts that one should reflect on often, whether one is . . . lay or ordained.

—UPAJJHATTHANA SUTTA, "THE FIVE REMEMBRANCES"

At the age of forty-four, Audre Lorde was diagnosed with breast cancer. It was 1978. Thus began a fifteen-year journey of living with chronic illness, the pain and insights of which she chronicled in two published journals and several essays. Lorde's willingness to share the many epiphanies that arose during her healing process continue to inform my own understanding of how to turn toward the reality of impermanence, how to live passionately in the face of death, and how to privilege self-care in the midst of illness.

"There Is Nothing Stable Under Heaven"

Illness, for Audre Lorde, was an opportunity to see the reality of impermanence more clearly. She observed, and began to appreciate, the fact of constant change. As she reflected on impermanence, she acknowledged the reality of inevitable decay and death. Refusing to accept the fact of impermanence makes pain worse, she acknowledged. There is inevitable change in life. "As a living creature I am part of two kinds of forces," she wrote, "growth and decay, sprouting and withering, living and dying, and at any given moment of our lives, each one of us is actively located somewhere along a continuum between these two forces."[1]

The terror Lorde experienced at the prospect of dying led her to write evocatively of impermanence. Writing was a practice of self-soothing. "I am learning to live beyond fear by living through it," Audre Lorde wrote in *The Cancer Journals*, "and in the process learning to turn fury at my own limitations into some more creative energy." She further reflected: "As women, we were raised to fear. If I cannot banish fear completely, I can learn to count with it less. For then fear becomes not a tyrant against which I waste my energy fighting, but a companion, not particularly desirable, yet one whose knowledge can be useful."[2] This theme—of the usefulness of feelings, regardless of how painful they are—surfaced consistently in Lorde's journals.

She stated in her introduction to *The Cancer Journals*—reflections that chronicle her experiences of undergoing a mastectomy in 1979—with the following words: "I am a post-mastectomy woman who believes our feelings need voice in order to be recognized, respected, and of use."[3]

For Lorde, the fear brought on by the ultimate experience of impermanence fostered an unflappable state of mind that could be applied to any situation, including that of political aggression. If she could turn toward the inevitability of death, she could turn toward the militarized onslaught against Black people, women, and lesbian and gay persons suffering mass violence throughout the world. In *The Cancer Journals*, she wrote: "If I can look directly at my life and my death without flinching, I know there is nothing they can ever do to me again."[4]

Looking directly at the human condition—the fact of impermanence, the reality of death—was a theme in James Baldwin's writings, too. His observations of the white world's avoidance of death fostered his reflections on the human condition and the nature of constant change.

Baldwin assessed that human beings think of themselves as having stable identities based on their social relations and their thoughts. He observed that white people's desire for permanence brought about a pathological pattern of denial. Indeed, Baldwin perceived, human beings are in a constant process of change, even if white people refuse to see it. Human thoughts and bodies are constantly in flux; so too is the world around them.

Baldwin recognized this fundamental truth in his essay "The Creative Process." He wrote:

> Society must accept some things as real; but [the artist] must always know that visible reality hides a deeper one, and that all our action and achievement rest on things unseen. A society must assume that it is stable, but the artist must know, and he must let us know, that there is nothing stable under heaven.[5]

Human authority, for Baldwin, arose from the capacity to face the facts of life—impermanence and death—including the suffering embedded in them. This was true with regard to material comfort as well. Acknowledging impermanence requires an embrace of emotional discomfort rather than privileging superficial appearances and luxury.

Baldwin cultivated the muscles to take on the pain inherent in impermanence. He sought to look directly at the pain embedded in the fact of constant change. In parsing the reality of impermanence, Baldwin encountered a natural law beyond the construction of race and sexuality. He wrote:

> It is the responsibility of free men to trust and to celebrate what is constant—birth, struggle, and death are constant, and so is love, though we may not always think so—and to apprehend the nature of change, to be able and willing to change. I speak of change not on the surface but in the depths—change in the sense of renewal. But renewal becomes impossible if one supposes things to be constant that are not—safety, for example, or money, or power.[6]

For Baldwin—and Lorde—the capacity to turn toward impermanence and death demonstrated a level of personal and spiritual maturity. Neither Baldwin nor Lorde suggested that Black people should suffer disproportionately. Yet acknowledging that "there is nothing stable under the sun" is a truth that encapsulates the world around us. When we acknowledge this truth, we can use it to grow. In their capacity to face the "conundrum" of impermanence and death—*and to live with passion*—Baldwin and Lorde illuminate the potential for liberation that is central to the Buddhist doctrine on impermanence and death.

Integrating Death into Living

Lorde's confrontation with the fact of impermanence and death inspired a wellspring of insights. She still experienced anxiety, but confronting the fact of death furthered her capacity to embrace her fear and use it for growth and change. On November 19, 1979, she wrote: "There must be some way to integrate death into living, neither ignoring it or giving into it."[7]

When Lorde was again diagnosed with cancer at age fifty—this time with cancer of the liver—the prospect of impending death impacted every aspect of her consciousness. But rather than resist it or repress debilitating feelings of terror, she sought to embrace the reality of her diagnosis and to work skillfully with the feelings that arose. This process was emotional even as it was practical. She embraced meditation and relaxed movement exercises, as well as natural therapies and healthy food.

Acceptance of impermanence and its ultimate marker, death, became a daily work, a constant practice of attuning to her body and making wise choices of how to care for herself. It required a practice of training her mind; she acknowledged that denying death would only lead to more suffering. She wrote: "I must let this pain flow through me and pass on. If I resist or try to stop it, it will detonate inside me, shatter me, splatter my pieces against every wall and person I touch."[8] The intensity of her desire to relax into the fear and pain conveyed her strength. Pain and fear would not be the last words.

The will to work on behalf of women, Black people, and gay and lesbian persons throughout the world—she traveled to Germany, France, Switzerland, the West Indies, and different regions of the United States in the last years of her life—was a driving force for Lorde. At the same time, she turned toward the implications of her liver cancer. She felt that all of her pain and terror could be used for service. On November 12, 1986, she reflected: "There is a terrible clarity that comes from living with cancer that can be empowering if we do not turn aside from it."[9] The "terrible clarity" expanded with a practice of accepting the fact of impending death, rather than pivoting from it.

That clarity and empowerment, for Lorde, was the awareness that even as she cared for her psyche and her body, she was most full of life when she surrounded herself with a community of loving women. She continued to assume her stance as a warrior. She wrote: "Battling racism and battling heterosexism and battling apartheid share the same urgency inside me as battling cancer."[10] The disproportionate violence and tragedy landing on Black women's backs ignited in Lorde a sense of constant struggle. The presence of cancer also implied combat. This struggle was both personal and political. She could identify an enemy and saw herself as a warrior in a fight that was also in her body. The enemy was disguised as illness; it operated in her cells as well as in the broader world. Lorde mused:

> How do I hold faith with sun in a sunless place? It is so hard not to counter this despair with a refusal to see. But I have to stay open and filtering no matter what's coming at me, because that arms me in a particular Black woman's way. When I'm open, I'm also less despairing. The more clearly I see what I'm up against, the more able I am to fight this process going on in my body that they're calling liver cancer. And I am determined to fight it even when I am not sure of the terms of the battle nor the face of victory. I just know I must not surrender my body to others unless I completely understand and agree with what they think should be done to it. I've got to look at all of my options carefully, even the ones I find distasteful. I know I can broaden the definition of winning to the point where I can't lose.[11]

She approached her cancer in a way that was familiar to her: She turned toward the possibilities of inner and outer change, which, she acknowledged, were "not easy nor quick."[12]

She acknowledged that she did not control many of the levers of her life. Nonetheless, she still possessed power: to choose how to meet the fact of pain, of death. She could not control the reality of cancer, but she could determine how to live passionately in the face of it.

As Lorde grappled with her grief and fear, she made significant choices that, in turn, brought her joy. After leaving a Swiss alternative treatment center in January 1986, she traveled to the West Indies. She wrote: "This is the year I spent spring beachcombing in St. Croix . . . a loving context in which I fit and thrive."[13] After moving to St. Croix in late 1986, she wrote about the lack of certainty in daily life amid the commitment to living as fully as possible. She reflected:

> I work, I love, I rest, I see and learn. And I report. These are my givens. Not sureties, but a firm belief that whether or not living them with joy prolongs my life, it certainly enables me to pursue the objectives of that life with a deeper and more effective clarity.[14]

The fact of impermanence and its final iteration, death, led Lorde to reflect on the difficulty of changing oneself even as feminists sought to dismantle racism, sexism, and homophobia in society. Lorde wrote: "I find myself always on guard against what is oversimplified, or merely cosmetic."[15] The wisdom that emerged from facing the depth of her suffering fostered a sense of curiosity about the changes taking place in her body.[16]

Her capacity to notice complexity arose from her practice of emotional self-scrutiny. Such examination, in turn, resulted in an articulation of myriad forms of power. In November 1986, Lorde wrote: "Living a self-conscious life, vulnerability as armor."[17]

Lorde went on to reflect: "Living fully—how long is not the point."[18]

This is also the message of the Buddhist teachings on impermanence. The fact that things end is a given, but as Lorde described, we can choose how to live in the midst of constant change.

Buddhism: The Five Remembrances

The Buddha taught that contemplating five subjects will help us to cultivate the path of wisdom and destroy obsessions. As quoted from the *Upajjhatthana Sutta* at the beginning of this chapter, we, as human beings, are subject to aging, illness, death, and separation. And lastly, we are the owners of our own actions. All beings are subject to these laws of nature. The *Upajjhatthana Sutta* continues:

> *Now, a disciple of the noble ones considers this: "I am not the only one subject to aging, who has not gone beyond aging. To the extent that there are beings—past and future, passing away and re-arising—all beings are subject to aging, have not gone beyond aging." When he/she often reflects on this, the [factors of the] path take birth. He/she sticks with that path, develops it, cultivates it. As he/she . . . [does so], the fetters are abandoned, the obsessions destroyed.*
>
> *Further, a disciple of the noble ones considers this: "I am not the only one subject to illness, who has not gone beyond illness.". . . "I am not the only one subject to death, who has not gone beyond death.". . . "I am not the only one who will grow different, separate from all that is dear and appealing to me."*[19]

In my own practice, I have leaned into the Five Remembrances, as they are known, as a path of wisdom. But I have needed Audre Lorde's voice, too, to remember that there is a broader view of illness, aging, and death. We are all subject to these laws. But sometimes illness descends too soon on some bodies that are seen as expendable by the broader culture. Lorde's biographer Alexis Pauline Gumbs ponders this at great length. Did Lorde get cancer because when she was eighteen years old and broke, she worked in a factory and was exposed to radioactive material? Furthermore, Gumbs notes that the workers in the factory were predominantly Black and Brown women.[20]

Lorde did not resist the fact of her illness and impending death. But she saw the burden of illness and death falling disproportionately on Black and Brown women. She named this pattern in apartheid South Africa as well as the United States. Old age, sickness, and death are inevitable for all of us. But some of us are considered expendable, and for us, old age, sickness, and death arrive too soon.

We have to protect ourselves, even as we seek to protect others, to balance stress with self-care and restoration. I heard this message in Lorde's reflections. It inspired me to rest.

"Caring for Myself Is Not Self-Indulgence, It Is Self-Preservation"

In the epilogue of her journals on living with liver cancer, Lorde wrote:

> I had to examine, in my dreams as well as in my immune-function tests, the devastating effects of overextension. Overextending is not stretching myself. I had to accept how difficult it is to monitor the difference. Necessary for me as cutting down on sugar. Crucial. Physically. Psychically. Caring for myself is not self-indulgence, it is self-preservation, and that is an act of political warfare.[21]

Lorde's rawness as she grappled with the implications of her illness have inspired my own activism, and that of countless women I know who are asked to do too much. Even as we seek to confront violence and alleviate suffering, we are reminded of the need for balance and self-care. Many of the women in my life struggle with constant exhaustion and burnout. It is both a state of mind and a result of overwhelming conditions; we are constantly responding to the magnitude of what is coming at us.

In my own life, I have taken on enormous responsibilities, often with little or no support. And while I have not been diagnosed with cancer, I have lived with chronic illness, so much so that Lorde's words have resonated with me for more than two decades.

I remembered her wisdom when I underwent a life-threatening illness at the age of thirty-five. I was parenting a one-year-old child and attempting to make my way through a doctoral program. The pressure was too much, literally. One afternoon after stepping off a flight following an academic conference, I noticed my head was throbbing. The pain was above my right ear. The following day, it had deepened into a migraine that did not go away. I stopped being able to eat or to sleep lying down. I saw doctors who could not help me. One day I managed to drive myself to the emergency room forty-five minutes away. The doctor gave me heavy painkillers and sent me home. But the migraine only deepened.

I stopped being able to speak clearly and could not swallow anything, even water. The next doctor I saw sent me to an Ear, Nose, and Throat specialist an hour away. This doctor put a camera down my throat and noticed that my soft palate and vocal cords were not moving correctly. He scheduled an MRI for that evening and admitted me to the hospital the next day.

"Two forces, growth and decay, sprouting and withering, living and dying," Lorde wrote.[22] I was decaying, withering, dying. The MRI results showed a five-inch blood clot that had formed next to my brain and was moving toward my chest. It had damaged my vagus nerve, which runs the length of the human torso. This damage, in turn, had partially paralyzed my voice box and soft palate. It was the reason I could not speak or eat.

The only good news from the diagnosis was that the clot had formed in a vein instead of an artery. If it had formed in an artery, I would have had a stroke, and likely permanent brain damage.

Every day was an act of grappling with severe physical pain and trying to not succumb to the terror of not knowing what was happening. The severity of the migraines threatened to buckle me. I held blocks of ice to my head throughout the day and fell asleep, when I could, with ice packs draped over my forehead. I heard Lorde's words much later when I reflected upon this period in my life: "One of the hardest things to accept is learning to live within uncertainty and neither deny it nor hide behind it. Most of all, to listen to the messages of uncertainty without allowing them to immobilize me, nor keep me from the certainties of those truths in which I believe."[23] What were those truths? To use all suffering for growth. To speak, even when I was afraid. Perhaps most importantly from that point forward, to practice self-care as an act of political warfare.

Practicing with Old Age, Sickness, and Death

We have to care for ourselves, especially as Black women. Our bodies and labor have historically been, and continue to be, viewed as expendable. We have to slow down when we are exhausted; we have to take time to rest. This was Lorde's message.

I *wanted* deep health. It had been more than fourteen years since I had experienced the blood clot. I still struggled with chronic illness. I asked my friend Karla Jackson-Brewer, a teacher in the Tara Mandala lineage, to guide me through a practice of impermanence and death. She suggested the Feeding Your Demons practice developed by her teacher, Lama Tsultrim Allione.

The day that I did a guided Feeding Your Demons practice, I was spent. This was my recipe for persistent illness—taxed adrenal glands and a depleted immune system. Suffering due to old age, sickness, and death, the Buddha said. I was aging very clearly. With advanced age came more aches and pains in my lower back; increased inflammation in my left shoulder, problems sleeping, a stiff neck. Anxiety reared its head, fed by numerous streams of thought: concern for my children, anguish at what was taking place politically. That anxiety was my demon.

Karla instructed me to set out two cushions facing each other. I closed my eyes and began to settle. I attuned to the pace of the hectic morning, of getting kids out of the door *on time*, of working through their resistance. Sitting was a welcome reprieve to the challenges of parenting.

Karla led me through a series of visualizations and questions. I first imagined a demon: large, covered in dark gray needles, composed of the black gunk that I unclogged from my bathroom drain whenever the sink stopped up. The demon was slimy and porous. It made demands of me: Take care of other people, meet deadlines. Its energy was perpetually anxious.

My demon needed too much from me: to keep working, to constantly keep things moving. Its message to me was: "You exist to make me happy, but you yourself do not matter. Your role in life is to pacify me." This was the voice that I had internalized, the voice of continually striving at the expense of my health and well-being. I had been born a Black girl into a white family, a white world. I was told, at the outset, that I existed to serve others.

The demon had few features. Its mouth was a hole. Its eyes were holes. There was a flatness to its appearance. Its spiky body was hard, inflexible, even as it consisted of porous muck. It had a male energy, even though I did not identify it as male. Its presence dominated; its voice was insistent, hard. I felt the energy drain from my body as I confronted the pressure that emanated from it. Just its messages— do more, meet this deadline, perform, serve me, your needs do not matter—led to a feeling of deep exhaustion. I did not have to actually be doing anything to feel the fatigue. I just had to hear the message to notice my body sag, to feel my throat itch with what seemed to be the beginnings of a cold.

I could feel in my body where the tension landed. My neck, just beneath my skull. It rippled down my neck to my shoulders, clenching my trapezoid muscles. They felt hard, like rocks.

I asked the demon three questions, beginning with:

What do you want?

To get all of my needs met. To feel loved. Energy.

I could feel my body relax just as I was able to answer this first question.

I asked, then:

What do you need?

To take care of myself. To be internally stable.

Finally, I queried:

How will you feel when you get what you really need?

A sense of well-being, of liberation. I will be clear like running water. Not stuck. More at ease.

After feeding the demon those feelings, it transformed into an ally: now deep golden yellow, soft rather than spiky. A refuge. The opposite of hard, insistent energy. It emanated relaxation; I could feel the entirety of my body being held. This ally, serene and velvety, told me:

I am here for you. I will ease your suffering.

This ally was female, maternal.

I will hold you when you are tired. I will give you time.

What do you need?

Time. Support. Spaciousness for deep practice.

How can I help you?

I need help in practical ways: picking up my kids from school, getting dinner on the table, cleaning my house. I need spaciousness around the hardness of deadlines.

Dead-lines. Pressure that suggests death.

The ally was golden, filled with sunlight.

I am here for you.

When I looked at her, instead of seeing flatness, I saw features: smiling eyes, full lips gently parted in a smile. The golden soft fur that covered her full body was reminiscent of land and water all at once. Fluid. And stable. Like a rippling mountain covered in brilliant green moss.

This ally evoked rest, refuge, a sense of stability, a place to land. I conjured her softness, her beauty, as a spaciousness within me. It was possible to let go and be held. I was not alone. Moreover, I was no longer marching to an external drumbeat. I was going to slow down. I was going to stand on my own terms.

Cultivating Fearlessness: Facing Death in Activism

Practices of self-care to heal illness, including visualization practices, cultivate mental stability and ease. And this peaceful energy, in turn, is extended outward toward our communities as we work to create conditions in which we can thrive.

Audre Lorde named the importance of self-care as she advocated for the rights of Black women in Germany, South Africa, and the United States, and as she advocated for the visibility of gay and lesbian persons worldwide. The work of uplifting marginalized persons was the work of standing against powers that attempt to enact annihilation on the most vulnerable populations in our world.

Challenging state violence, even while simultaneously confronting illness and impending death, was lifelong work for Lorde.

This was also true for Baldwin, who honored the fearless Black civil rights and Black Power activists who looked death in the face—by facing police officers with batons and giving themselves over to arrest. He wrote to Angela Y. Davis during her imprisonment and visibly supported Black Power activists during events and fundraisers. He hailed the civil rights heroes of the South who marched with fortitude against fire hoses and snarling dogs trained on them by city officials. These activists insisted on their humanity and rights despite the virulent hatred of white Southerners and hostile Northerners. These fearless Black children and parents embodied a capacity to face death and embrace the consequences of challenging the status quo.

Baldwin saw this stamina in the figure of fifteen-year-old Dorothy Counts, who was one of four Black high schoolers (each enrolled at different schools) determined to fight segregation in their home city of Charlotte, North Carolina. Counts integrated Harding High School *by herself*, even in the face of threats, physical attacks, and humiliation. This kind of commitment to social justice required a willingness to face death, including the fear of death, Baldwin observed. As a "witness" to the civil rights movement, Baldwin observed that Black people would risk everything, even their lives, to achieve justice for their people. To dismantle oppression and fight for one's community required facing death for the sake of an expansive, comprehensive freedom.[24]

We enter the movement for social change with whatever we have to offer. For Baldwin and Lorde, the commitment to movement work flowed from their writing. "Freedom is a constant struggle," Angela Y. Davis stated.[25] This was true for Baldwin and Lorde. As they faced their own deaths—both from liver cancer—they simultaneously worked on behalf of Black people's freedom worldwide.[26] They both saw, in collective uprisings, oppressed people's willingness to face death in their refusal to back down from state violence.

The willingness to face death requires inner fortitude. It requires rest. Baldwin saw this starkly as he observed the grassroots civil rights activists who faced screaming mobs and were terrorized and denied due process simply because they insisted upon respect. He mourned the deaths of his friends, Medgar Evers, Malcolm X, and Martin Luther King Jr., as he attempted to write about their integrity in his unfinished

manuscript *Remember This House*. In pondering his friends' willingness to face death, he sought to answer a lurking question: What was
it about these figures that led them into the fray so that they put their
bodies in the line of fire with unfailing commitment? He honored their
unflinching stamina.

Facing mortality directly requires building emotional muscles
and an ability to believe in the interconnectedness of all beings.
Audre Lorde wrote of the rising and falling of the nature of life and
the relationship between growth and decay. She grappled with the
fact of death by attempting to live in the present, giving all of her
energies to the necessary work of political and psychological liberation. Lorde saw these different facets of liberation as intertwined:
Liberating the mind and heart was inseparable from creating community, inseparable from supporting the liberation of Black South
African women from the shackles of apartheid.[27] The work was the
same. To focus only on one aspect of liberation was to dismiss how
layers of oppression function within a complex society. For Baldwin—
who died in 1987 at age sixty-three—the capacity to face death was
as much an interior, self-reflective process as it was an exterior one.
Even as he suffered poor health and was eventually immobilized by
illness, Baldwin honored rituals of community and courage: breaking bread at "the welcome table" as well as putting one's body in the
line of fire during a protest, risking arrest and imprisonment, and
taking bullets for one's people.[28]

For Baldwin and Lorde—and the Buddha—facing mortality arose
from a direct capacity to see the transient nature of life clearly and to
hone in on what mattered most to them. As they turned toward their
grief and honored their rage, they simultaneously became less afraid of
death. Their fearlessness fueled their capacity to reach outside themselves and attune to the people they loved most and the suffering of
those in different parts of the world. Fearlessness fed connection and
compassion. Baldwin and Lorde, in reckoning with death, became less

attached to their own particular lives and more connected to those whose suffering arose from oppressive conditions. Existence was fleeting; it was also valuable, not to be ignored, dismissed, or denied. Life was to be honored but not attached to, respected but not clung to. Taking into account the fact of impermanence, confronting with passion the fact of death, and practicing self-care in the midst of illness made them freer to offer their lives to others and for others.

PRACTICE
Feeding Your Demons

The "Feeding Your Demons" practice in the Tara Mandala lineage is one that I have found useful for working skillfully with illness and cultivating stamina in social justice activism.[29] Although individuals can do the practice themselves, Tara Mandala states that individuals should not use the practice on others unless they have been properly certified in the method. To prepare, set out two cushions, facing one another, so that you can move back and forth as you meditate.

THE FIVE STEPS
Step 1. Find the Demon

Choose the demon or god—for example, fear or anger—with which you want to work.

Thinking about this demon, perhaps remembering a particular time or incident when it presented itself. Scan your body and locate where you are holding this demon most strongly.

Notice the following:

Where is the demon?

What is its shape?

What is its color?

What is its texture?

What is its temperature?

Now intensify this sensation.

Step 2. Personify the Demon and Find Out What It Needs

Now allow this sensation, color, texture, and temperature to move out of your body and become personified in front of you as a being with limbs, a face, eyes, and so on. (If an inanimate object appears in your mind, imagine what it would look like if it were personified as some kind of animate being.)

Notice the following about the demon:

Size

Color

Surface of its body

Density

Smell, if any

Sounds, if any

Gender, if it has one

The look in its eyes

Its emotional state

Its character

Something about the demon you did not see before

Now ask the demon the following questions:

What do you want?

What do you really need?

How will you feel when you get what you really need?

Switch places (sit on the cushion or chair facing yours), keeping your eyes closed as much as possible.

Step 3. Become the Demon

Take a moment to settle into the demon's body. Adopt the posture or gesture of the demon if it is helpful.

Notice how it feels to be in the demon's body.

Notice how your normal self looks from the demon's point of view.

Answer the questions you asked in Step 2, speaking as the demon:

What I want is . . .

What I really need is . . .

When I get what I really need, I will feel . . . (Be sure to take note of this answer.)

Now return to your original seat.

Step 4. Feed the Demon and Meet the Ally

First, feed the demon.

Take a moment to settle back into your own body. See the demon opposite you.

Now evoke within your own body the feeling(s) that the demon said it would have when it gets what it really needs (the answer to the third question). Allow the feeling(s) to spread throughout your entire body. Then dissolve your body into nectar. The nectar has the quality of the feeling that the demon would have when it gets what it really needs (i.e., the answer to the third question).

Notice the color of the nectar.

Feed the demon this nectar and notice how the demon takes it in.

An infinite supply of nectar flows to the demon. Feed the demon until it's completely satisfied. This can take some time. If the demon seems insatiable, imagine how it would look if it were completely satisfied.

Now it's time to meet the ally.

Notice if a being is present after the demon is completely satisfied. If there is, ask this being if it is the ally. If it is not, invite an ally to appear. Likewise, if no being is present after you finish feeding the demon to its complete satisfaction, invite an ally to appear.

Notice all the details of the ally: its color, its size, and the look in its eyes.

When you really feel connected with the energy of the ally, ask these questions:

How will you help me?

How will you protect me?

What pledge do you make to me?

How can I access you?

Change places and become the ally. Take a moment to settle into the ally's body. Adopt the posture or gesture of the ally if it is helpful. Notice how it feels to be in the ally's body. Notice how your normal self looks from the ally's point of view.

When you are ready, answer the questions you asked, speaking as the ally.

I will help you by . . .

I will protect you by . . .

I pledge I will . . .

You can access me by . . .

Notice if there is something else the ally would like to say.

Then return to your original seat.

Take a moment to settle back into your own body and see the ally opposite you. See the ally in front of you, look into its eyes, and feel its energy pouring into your body.

As you feel the energy of the ally coming into your body, feel it spread all the way down to the soles of your feet, to your fingertips, and throughout your whole body. Notice how this feels.

Now imagine that the ally dissolves into light. Notice the color of this light. Feel this light dissolving into you; integrate this luminosity into every cell of your body, as though all your cells were being bathed in light. Take note of the feeling of the integrated energy of the ally in your body.

Now you, with the integrated energy of the ally, dissolve.

Step 5. Rest

Rest in the state that is present after the dissolution, just rest.

Pause until discursive thoughts begin again. Now gradually come back to your body recalling the feeling of the energy of the ally.

As you open your eyes, maintain the feeling of the energy of the ally in your body.

It Comes from Somewhere

Eye consciousness does not say, "I am produced by these conditions," yet the eye consciousness is born due to the presence of these conditions.

—RICE SEEDLING SUTRA

Making the connections between illness and the broader social conditions that drive it has been a lifelong practice. So, too, has been making the connections between overdrive and my own underlying psychological patterns: the fears of rejection, the desire to be noticed and embraced. James Baldwin's observations of white American culture—particularly, the manifold delusions that uphold ideas of supremacy—have provided clarity and sustenance for my commitment to rewiring my ingrained anxieties and habits.

The Delusion of White Supremacy

As I attained inner stability through Buddhist practice, I became better equipped to stand back and observe the worldview of my mother's parents. I remembered their absurd, harmful actions with utter precision. When I was twelve, they told me to my face that my brother and I were mistakes. On one occasion, when my brother was little, my grandparents kept him in their house and their back-yard for a week; they did not allow my brother to leave the prem-ises. This was during a period in which my mother needed help with childcare. They were willing to provide the practical support, but they had not wanted their neighbors to know that my brother was staying with them.

I was in college when I finally erupted. My grandparents had thrown a fiftieth wedding anniversary party for themselves and had told my mother not to bring us if she and her white husband chose to attend. Even extended family members were not supposed to know of our existence. They had said to my uncle, "we can't get past the skin" and had written to my mother stating flatly, "we are not going to air your dirty laundry in public." When I confronted them, upon learning of the celebration just months after I graduated, they defended them-selves. "We must know a hundred people," my grandmother told me. "None of *them* have Black grandchildren!"

At the time, I was hurt, confused. Enraged. But gradually, I was able to detach from their harmful behavior. Rather than circling around their judgment cautiously, I found myself thinking of them as morally vacant. I was still outraged. And yet. Reading James Baldwin helped me understand their delusion.

"This Is a Curiously and Dangerously Fragmented Society"

My mother's parents, in all of their white pretentiousness and social climbing, sought to "become white" as first-generation Eastern Euro-pean immigrants. They were Slavic, seen as inferior in contrast to Western European newcomers. My grandfather, as the breadwinner, was relegated to separate social spheres in the workplace. He knew that he was looked down upon because he was Slavic, he told me once.

As a young man, before he adopted a white racial identity, he claimed an ethnic one.

Over the course of his lifetime, that changed. He and my grandmother, who spoke Czech and Slovak at home, moved from Cicero, Illinois, to the Western suburbs of Chicago, where their ethnic identities mattered less than their whiteness. They joined several social clubs to support their hobbies as they aspired to belong to their middle-class suburban world. As they disassociated from their ethnic roots and adopted a white racial identity, they continued to look down on Black people. Cicero—the suburb in which they had raised my mother—was a sundown town. Black people could work but not live there. The suburb to which they moved later in life—in which they would not let my brother leave the house and the backyard for fear that the neighbors would see him—was similarly an all-white enclave.

Baldwin clarified the cost of their assimilation. The fact that white immigrants could not acknowledge the price of their white racial ticket resulted in enormous, consequential suffering. Baldwin stated in his 1984 essay, "On Being White . . . and Other Lies," that when white people give up their past, it results in weakness and powerlessness. Without a real past, white people only possess invented myths.[1]

This collective delusion goes unacknowledged by white people in positions of authority who benefit from centering white voices—from Hollywood films to elementary school history books.[2] Baldwin deconstructed the immorality underlying white ideals, pointing to the delusions embedded in constant grasping toward white innocence and material wealth.

White people in the United States avoid "stink," Baldwin argued.[3] Avoiding stink—and the resulting myopia about everyone else's suffering—is rooted in a process of white identity construction.

Baldwin stated in a 1986 interview:

There is a curiously and dangerously fragmented society while, perhaps unlike any society in the past, it has all the stirrings of well-being. It has at its back the resonance of the American Dream and the history of conquest. But it is also based on a lie, the lie of Manifest Destiny. So it's a country immobilized, with a past it cannot explain away . . . Everybody has something to hide, and when you have to hide, you have to cry for despair. Despair is the American crime. So one is trapped in a kind of Sunday purgatory, and the only way out of that is to confront what you are afraid of. The American image of the black face contains everything America most wants and everything that terrifies it. It also contains the castrations, the lynchings, the burnings, the continual daily and hourly debasements of life, and you cannot do those things without doing something to yourself.[4]

I saw this embrace of lies in my relationship with my grandparents. They resisted the circumstances of my birth: that I was born as a result of a sexual relationship between their daughter, a white woman, and a Black man. I saw, too, their fear of death and their association of Black with anything that they considered defiled. They sneered at predominantly Black public housing units in Chicago. They put plastic on their living room couches. They denied my existence. Anything associated with dirt was to be rejected.

They had built their lives in a myopic bubble. It was hateful. It was deluded. Over time, I saw their evasion through Baldwin's eyes. Their rejection of my Blackness was morally repugnant, not worth emulating. And yet, I heard Baldwin say, it could not be ignored. White people's avoidance resulted in tangible consequences for Black people. It was worthwhile, Baldwin felt, to understand the "white problem."[5] I understood Baldwin's desire to understand the white mind as I considered my own psychological patterns, and as I learned about my father's life.

My father was a man who was sporadically in my life until I was seven years old. I do not remember him well. I am told he was charming and empathic, but I have only a few memories. The most salient one is of walking down the street with him, our hands clasped together, and comparing the lightness of my brown skin with his darker hue. I watched him meet my younger brother for the first time that day. My brother, who was one year old, was fearful, unwilling to be held by a man he did not know.

That was the last time I saw my father.

My father's absence was familiar, normal. I did not, at a young age, understand it negatively. It was only in my early adolescence that I began to internalize my father's absence as rejection.

I attempted to understand him. My father's life had been difficult from a young age. The conditions of a Black boy born in Chicago in 1947 were what Baldwin described as the "incessant and gratuitous humiliation and danger one encountered every working day, all day long."[6] Baldwin was talking about Harlem, but it was not different from the South Side. My father had lived in a segregated part of the city, a formerly white neighborhood that had absorbed Black migrants fleeing sharecropping and Jim Crow segregation. The South Side, like Harlem, contained rat-infested slum housing that was egregiously expensive. Store products were much more costly than in wealthier neighborhoods. Police stood on every corner, watching, brutalizing.

In writing about Harlem, Baldwin articulated my father's existence.

The sorrow, rage, and defeat that Baldwin described had permeated my father's childhood. These conditions complicated my feelings for him. I had been hurt by him, but I could also put into perspective all that he had endured. I knew very little. But I knew enough.

My father was perhaps eight years old when his parents separated. His father had migrated north with several siblings from Friars Point, Mississippi, an all-Black town on the Mississippi River. His mother, too, had gone north during the Great Migration as she followed her brothers out of the Mississippi Delta. My father's parents met in

Chicago. When they separated, he and two siblings were sent to live with relatives. It was an unstable childhood in a city that grew rapidly, with difficulty, as Black migrants moved into it from the rural South. This much I knew.

I do not know if my father finished high school. I do know that, at the age of eighteen, he fathered a child. At some point during this time, he developed an addiction to heroin. He married and had another child. When my mother met him, he was traveling to a methadone clinic several times a week.

"They Know They Are Afraid of Something"

It was not hard to feel into the devastation that Baldwin—born just twenty-three years earlier than my father, also on August 2—described. That my father and Baldwin shared a birth date and, from all accounts, charisma, was present for me. Perhaps in some way, Baldwin assumed the voice of a fatherly guide in my mind. I could hear the intensity of his reflection on white people's mentality, the sustained attention he gave toward discerning their worldview. He wanted to understand what drove their hatred of Black people. Baldwin's capacity to see through white arrogance resulted in his refusal to take on white people's expectations. He found white society immoral, pretentious, sickening. White apathy allowed Black poverty to fester. There was no excuse for it.

For Baldwin, there was no such thing as a "Negro problem" or "Black problem." The problem was white people who constructed and scapegoated Black people as inferior. To dispel their delusion, to tear down their myths, Baldwin argued that white people needed to do their own interior work, to understand themselves and their motivations for seeking comfort and constructing illusions at the expense of Black people's lives. White Americans needed to confront their internal conditioning, their insecurities and shame.

On this note, perhaps most extensively, he wrote on the delusions of white people who pretended to uphold democratic and Christian moral values but refused to examine themselves and their society.

> People who cling to their delusions find it difficult, if not impossible, to learn anything worth learning: a people under the necessity of creating themselves must examine everything, and soak up learning the way the roots of a tree soak up water. A people still held in bondage must believe that *Ye shall know the truth and the truth shall set you free.*[7]

Even as Black people suffered from external oppression and internalized racism, in Baldwin's eyes, it was white people who needed liberating. In his testimony before Congress to establish a commission on Negro culture, Baldwin argued that "[White people] are frightened. I don't hate white people; I don't have to. I am not afraid of you. You face a Southern deputy, and he *does* hate you—because he is scared to death of you. He is the one who is in trouble, and that is the man you have to liberate."[8] In his essay "In Search of a Majority," assuming the voice of white people, Baldwin wrote:

> In a way, if the Negro were not here, we might be forced to deal within ourselves and our own personalities, with all those vices, all those conundrums, and all those mysteries with which we have invested the Negro race . . .

He continued in his own voice:

> They [white people] do not really know what they are afraid of, but they know they are afraid of something, and they are so frightened that they are nearly out of their minds. And this same fear obtains on one level or another, to varying degrees throughout the entire country.[9]

Baldwin stated that the white people who would ostensibly never allow Black people "to starve, to grow bitter, and to die in ghettos" were the same white people who repressed the unnamable fear that they projected onto Black bodies. He argued that official government reports are conducted not to illuminate data and facts, but rather, to obscure information about Black people who are represented by statistics. Elevating numbers, not Black humanity, leads to evasion. As a result, Baldwin said, white people can maintain their delusion.

For all of these reasons, Baldwin dismissed white moral pretentiousness. But he did not dismiss the harm caused by white delusion. Black people suffered a cataclysmic pain that was passed down generationally. I felt that. I had been hurt by my father, but I was aware, too, that his absence was a result of forces beyond his control. He had been subjected to horrific conditions; his parents, too, in their instability, had also endured hostile environments. In Mississippi, segregation was the law of the land and lynchings were the norm. My father's people had been sharecroppers in a southern state that had been deemed the most violent, the most lawless of them all.[10] My father himself was not far removed from the terrorism of the white South; he was, at the same time, exposed to the cruelty of the white North.

My father had abandoned me. I did not excuse the harm that he had caused. But I did recognize the conditions that undergirded his rejection of me; I did recognize that he had been conditioned by the poverty and violence in Chicago. Baldwin helped me see more clearly how these conditions were a consequence of white avoidance and delusion.

"It Is Hard to Be Black, and Therefore Officially, and Lethally, Despised."

White avoidance and delusion were a "white problem" that arose from childishness, the avoidance of suffering, Baldwin observed.

In his 1962 book *The Fire Next Time*, Baldwin reflected on the violent, impoverished conditions in Harlem that went unquestioned by white America. He discussed the internalization of poverty and isolation by young Black adolescents and the constant violence that Black people were required to confront. "Crime became real, for example—for the first time—not as *a* possibility but as *the* possibility," Baldwin wrote. Black people did not have options for sustaining themselves. Baldwin explained:

> School began to reveal itself, therefore, as a child's game that one could not win, and boys dropped out of school and went to work. My father wanted me to do the same. I refused, even though I no longer had any illusions about what an education could do for me; I had already encountered too many college-graduate handymen. My friends were now "downtown," busy, as they put it, "fighting the man." They began to care less about the way they looked, the way they dressed, and things they did; presently, one found them in twos and threes and fours, in a hallway, sharing a jug of wine or a bottle of whiskey, talking, cursing, fighting, sometimes weeping: lost, and unable to say what it was that oppressed them, except that they knew it was "the man"—the white man. And there seemed to be no way whatever to remove this cloud that stood between them and the sun, between them and love and life and power, between them and whatever it was that they wanted. One did not have to be very bright to realize how little one could do to change one's situation.[11]

As Baldwin shone a spotlight on the conditions of Black America— the de facto segregation in the Northern ghettos and de jure segregation in Southern Jim Crow towns—he emphasized how those degrading conditions impacted the psychological conditioning of Black people.

> This past, the Negro's past, of rope, fire, torture, castration, infanticide, rape; death and humiliation; fear by day and night, fear as deep as the marrow of the bone; doubt that he was worthy of life, since everyone around him denied it; sorrow for his women, for his kinfolk, for his children, who needed his protection, and whom he could not protect; rage so deep that it often turned against him and his own, and made all love, all trust, all joy impossible.[12]

The devastation that Baldwin described arises from the poverty and exploitation, from the violence and humiliations, that are ignored by white people. These conditions have real consequences. They distort Black people's individual and collective consciousnesses. They fuel despair, rage. They spark the impulse to "inspire fear" to protect one's body and one's family. Baldwin observed that these conditions make love and trust and joy inaccessible, out of reach. It was this despairing state of mind with which Baldwin was ultimately concerned. He wrote numerous essays on the psychological plight of Black people.[13] He identified the manifold ways in which we are taught to loathe ourselves.

In an essay on the sorrow songs, Baldwin stated bluntly: "It is hard to be black, and therefore officially, and lethally, despised."[14] Combing through the rubble of internalized racism—the ways in which Black people are taught to despise ourselves—Baldwin said, was more important than dismantling the material representations of power: guns, fleets, and bombs.[15] If white people paid the price of being white by giving up their histories and immigrant identities, Black people paid the price by seeking to be accepted by white people and by giving in to self-hatred.[16]

For Baldwin personally, the process of excavating internalized loathing and arriving at a deep sense of inner security could only take place after he left the United States and turned toward the blues, jazz, and the sorrow songs. In 1979, he reflected: "[In France] . . . I spoke no French. I dropped into a silence in which I heard, for the first time, the beat of the language of the people who had produced me. For the first time, I was able to hear that music."[17] He would return to the meaning of the blues and jazz in his fiction and essays over the next several decades.[18]

For Baldwin, who remained close to his mother and siblings throughout his life, turning toward the culture of Black people brought him closer to the complexity of being human. He wrote evocatively of love and the tremendous force of recognition, connection, and respect that comes from embracing one's own sorrow in Black music and art. The ability to embrace one's suffering, Baldwin argued, correspondingly fosters an ability to embrace another's suffering. In stripping away delusions and in rejecting myths and pretenses, genuine love is possible and, indeed, actualized. "Love takes off the masks that we fear we cannot live without and know we cannot live within. I use the word 'love' here not merely in the personal sense but as a state of being, or a state of grace—not in the infantile American sense of being made happy but in the tough and universal sense of quest and daring and growth," he wrote.[19]

To Black people, then, whose sense of identity was distorted by white delusion but who lived with the possibility of inner freedom, Baldwin spoke his message clearly: Black people attain "authority . . . that is unshakable."[20] Because Black people cannot avoid their suffering, Baldwin argued, they develop the capacity to see through delusion and identify it as the root of their suffering. Black people possess the strength and stamina to endure an environment in which the people in charge refuse to grow up. He implored Black people to reject the masks that they might be compelled to put on. If Black people embraced their pain, they could in turn stay close to joy and to one other. Baldwin stated in a 1973 interview with *The Black Scholar:*

> History was someone you touched, you know, on Sunday mornings or in the barbershop. It's all around you. It's in the music, it's in the way you talk, it's in the way you cry, it's in the way you make love. Because you are denied your official history, you are forced to excavate your real history even though you can never say that's what you are doing. That is what you are doing. That is one of the reasons for the lifestyle of Black Americans, which is a real lifestyle as distinguished from the total anonymity of white Americans who have so much history, all of which they believe. They are absolutely choked with it. They can't move because all the lies that they have told themselves, they actually think is their history.[21]

Baldwin's love for Black people did not mean that he always thought of Black people as wise, good, and courageous. He wondered what would happen when Black people, collectively, were no longer forced to constantly contend with white delusion.[22] He acknowledged that Black people routinely and often cruelly hurt one another, acknowledging that he himself wanted to murder Black adults who sell narcotics to children.[23] He observed that Black people, like white people, seek to embrace myths and create false origins, arguing in *The Fire Next Time* that the Nation of Islam and the Black Church are two institutions that have employed false myths of origin that would ultimately crack.

Yet—even as he refused to essentialize Blackness—Baldwin pointed out that the conditions in Black America were such that Black people could never escape the intensity of their plight. And in their inability to evade suffering, Black people possess insight into white delusion and the conditions it perpetuates.

Causes and Conditions

The Buddhist doctrine of "causes and conditions" illuminates Baldwin's analysis of the physical conditions created by white America, and as a result, how Black people *and* white people are mentally conditioned. Baldwin points to a fearful evasion on the part of white people that drives the cycle of oppressive conditions and consequent conditioning. This cycle is affirmed in Buddhist teachings.

The Buddhist doctrine of "causes and conditions" states, in brief, that everything we humans experience—the conditions that shape our consciousness—arises from ignorance. Our greed, hatred, and delusion— our mental suffering—comes from somewhere.

This doctrine is illuminated in the *Rice Seedling Sutra*, which tells the story of the bodhisattva Maitreya, an enlightened being who stayed on earth, among unenlightened humans, to support their liberation.[24]

Maitreya begins his teaching with the fact of ignorance, the first link of twelve on the "causes and conditions" chain. Ignorance is not simply the absence of knowledge. It is a form of delusion—that is, wrongful thinking.[25] It is a cognitive action. It leads to ingrained thought patterns that shape character. Think of a mental train track running in a loop. Our intellect functions the same way, leading to perceptions and ideas that become thought patterns—train tracks—in our minds. Internal conditions—ignorance, greed, hatred, and delusion—determine whether mental formations and deluded consciousness arise.

Or think of external conditions—earth, water, fire, wind, and space— that determine whether something will arise. A flower blooms because of the kind of soil it is planted in, whether it receives enough rain, and the amount of sun it can take in. The same is true of external conditions such as poverty, warfare, and racism.

Maitreya points out that as a result of the first link—ignorance—a second link is formed. This link consists of mental formations: habitual and conditioned ways of thinking, states of mind through which we are predisposed to filter all experiences. These mental formations, in turn, lead to the third link in the twelve-link chain: consciousness, "that which knows."[26] This consciousness is conditioned by ignorance, and therefore deluded.

The *Rice Seedling Sutra* speaks about internalized narratives as stories that arise from ignorance, thought patterns, and deluded consciousness. It identifies ignorance as belief in the idea that any phenomenon is constant. For example, deluded consciousness is thinking that narratives of white supremacy are true, or that they are permanent.

"Life Is Tragic"

Ignorance and deluded consciousness impact (condition) our external environments—the waters we swim in. This idea is central to Buddhist doctrine; it is also central to Baldwin's thought.

Even as Baldwin was concerned with the degraded conditions and internal conditioning of Black people, he gave equal weight to the ways in which white delusion impacts white consciousness.

One aspect of white delusion is to avoid the fact of death and project the fear of death onto Black bodies. White people choose to evade their fear of death and instead buy into the myths that pervade white America, Baldwin argued. Yet, he said, the lies are brittle and certain to fall apart. The myths are unstable. And the desire to hide behind them, and resist reality, perpetuates deluded conditions.

I observed this phenomenon with my white grandparents. They bought into the myth of white superiority; they projected their emotional limitations onto my father's Black body, my own Black body. My father and I represented, for them, shame and danger, something unwanted. Isolation. Death.

Baldwin's observations of white Americans' avoidance of death is for me one of the most compelling aspects of his analysis on how race functions in the United States. He spent a great deal of time thinking about white people's worldviews, and why they cling to the color of their skin with such ferocity. He was puzzled and not at all impressed by white delusions of morality. It seemed to Baldwin that white people like to think of themselves as good and moral, but cannot actually see the world as it is. They do not attempt to cultivate the stamina to face hardship and pain, including death. Their refusal to deal with their pain is infantile, childlike, Baldwin observed. Rather than grow up, they choose to blame Black people for their suffering. In their fear of death, they project their avoidance onto Black bodies.

Baldwin's analysis was abundantly clear to me when I reflected on my grandparents' racism. When I was nineteen years old, having observed once again that they refused to put photos of me in their living room—a place in their home in which their Black grandchild would be visible to their friends—I wrote them a letter acknowledging that I knew they were ashamed of me. They wrote back telling me that I did not help wash the dishes.

They were fundamentally avoidant. And clearly, they correlated my dark skin with servitude. My grandparents' refusal to acknowledge their racism, and the shame that lay beneath it, was part of a larger mentality, what the Caribbean philosopher Charles W. Mills referred to as "epistemological ignorance." In his 1997 book *The Racial Contract,* Mills wrote:

> One has an agreement to *mis*interpret the world. One has to learn to see the world wrongly, but with the assurance that this set of mistaken perceptions will be validated by white epistemic authority, whether religious or secular . . . producing the ironic outcome that whites will in general be unable to understand the world that they themselves have made.[27]

For Baldwin, choosing to see the world wrongly is not just a lack of knowledge. It is a lack of courage. Choosing to see the world *as it is* requires the capacity to take risks. It requires stamina, a willingness to confront ignorance and delusion. In Baldwin's eyes, the white Americans who face the verity of death are few and far between. Baldwin recognized death as a fact of life; it is central to the human experience. Baldwin also saw that it is natural to experience fear in light of old age, sickness, and death.

These are core teachings of the Buddha. The hagiography of the Buddha relates the story of a young prince, Siddhartha Gotama, who ventured out of his father's palace gates for the first time at the age of twenty-nine. On his journey, he witnessed human beings in different stages of decay: an old man clearly in decline, a sick person lying on the side of the road, and a corpse. Siddhartha Gotama came to the conclusion that nothing human beings do can negate the phenomenon of old age, sickness, and death. These are realities of the human condition, and therefore inescapable—but the suffering that arises from them should be taken seriously. Siddhartha Gotama then embarked upon a seven-year pilgrimage of fasting and ascetic practices. But extreme self-deprivation did not foster mental liberation. Rather, Siddhartha Gotama became enlightened under the Bodhi tree as he faced his suffering—known as *mara*—while calling upon the earth for support. Only then, legend tells us, was he able to see the transient nature of reality clearly.

This kind of aptitude requires the will to train the mind to see the impermanence of existence. It requires support. But, Baldwin said, Americans—specifically white Americans—refuse to embark upon this difficult path, nor do they create the conditions to facilitate attaining awareness. Instead, he argued, white Americans avoid and repress their aversion to mortality. In their quest to avoid their horror at the fact of death, they cannot say "yes" to life. He wrote:

> Now, in this country, this inability to say yes to life is part of our dilemma . . . of being what is known as an American. The collective effort until this moment, and the collective delusion until this moment, has been precisely my delusion when I was a little boy: that you could get what you wanted, and become what you said you were going to be, painlessly.[28]

The refusal to grow up—including the ability to confront the fact of death—is not only immature, Baldwin argued. It is also exploitative. For Baldwin, avoiding inevitable demise undergirds the centuries-old perpetuation of white delusion. In projecting their fear of death onto Black people, white people expect Black people to serve as receptacles of white people's repressed horrors.

> The difference between a boy and a man is that a boy imagines there is some way to get through life safely, and a man knows he's got to pay his dues. In this country, the entire nation has always assumed that I would pay their dues for them. What it means to be a Negro in this country is that you represent, you are the receptacle for and the vehicle of, all the pain, disaster, sorrow which white Americans think they can escape. This is

what is really meant by keeping the Negro in his place. It is why white people, until today, are still astounded and offended if, by some miscalculation, they are forced to suspect that you are not happy where they have placed you.[29]

Baldwin argued that white people need Black people to stay in their place, like a star in relation to a planet, so that they can perpetuate their avoidant, immature worldview. But this childlike evasion not only means that Black people remain receptacles of all that is unwanted—the stink, the fact of death—in the white world; it also means that white people cannot live life fully.

For Baldwin, human life is to be lived fully, in all of its devastation—including death—as well as in all of its joy. When they avoid the reality of death, white people cannot experience life "with passion."

As he assumed a white person's voice, Baldwin argued:

Our good will, from which we yet expect such power to transform us, is thin, passionless, strident: its roots, examined, lead us back to our forebears, whose assumption it was that the black man, to become truly human and acceptable, must first become like us. This assumption once accepted, the Negro in America can only acquiesce in the obliteration of his own personality, the distortion and debasement of his own experience, surrendering to those forces which reduce the person to anonymity and which make themselves manifest daily all over the darkening world.[30]

In order for white delusion to be maintained, Baldwin was saying, Black people must buy into it. But Black people are not easily or inevitably swayed. Black activists worldwide have made similar observations about the myth of white morality. This collective analysis gained traction in the 1960s and 1970s during decolonial movements throughout the globe, including on the continent of Africa. Opponents of settler colonialism deconstructed colonial narratives. These decolonial activists observed the contradictions of white people who evaded hard truths, and at the same time, projected themselves as saviors. In one example, the anti-apartheid activist Steve Biko indicted white liberals who professed to be on the side of Black South Africans. Biko wrote in 1970:

> A game at which the liberals have become masters is that of deliberate evasiveness. The question often comes up "what can I do?" If you ask him to do something like stopping to use seg-regated facilities or dropping out of varsity to work at menial jobs like all blacks or defying and denouncing all provisions that make him privileged, you always get the answer—"but that's unrealistic!"[31]

I concurred with Baldwin and Biko's analyses of the hollowness of white morality. The white people who believed in their own good-ness, while failing to do the hard work of seeing their role in upholding systems built on white delusion, wanted praise but not critique. This obvious pattern of seeking approval but avoiding hard truths contra-dicted their claims of upholding their own moral standards. I saw this pattern up close with my grandparents. They thought of themselves as good, and my father, my mother (who had transgressed racial bound-aries), and me as polluted. But their obvious racism contradicted their profession of goodness. I believed Baldwin when he argued:

> Behind what we think of as the Russian menace lies what we do not wish to face, and what white Americans do not face when they regard a Negro: reality—the fact that life is tragic. Life is tragic simply because the earth turns and the sun inexorably rises and sets, and one day, for each of us, the sun will go down for the last, last time. Perhaps the whole root of our trouble, the human trouble, is that we will sacrifice all the beauty of our lives, will imprison ourselves in totems, taboos, crosses, blood sacri-fices, steeples, mosques, races, armies, flags, nations, in order to deny the fact of death, which is the only fact we have. It seems to me that one ought to rejoice in the *fact* of death—ought to decide, indeed, to *earn* one's death by confronting with passion

the conundrum of life. One is responsible to life: It is the small beacon in that terrifying darkness from which we come and to which we shall return. One must negotiate this passage as nobly as possible, for the sake of those who are coming after us. But white Americans do not believe in death, and this is why the darkness of my skin so intimidates them.[32]

I sat with Baldwin's words. The avoidance of death, on the part of white people, perpetuates an environment of antagonism and violence. White people cannot control the fact of death. But they *can* control Black bodies, which represent death. And they will do everything they can to maintain that control, and the delusion that bolsters it.

"You Got Upset. And Now You Must Ask Yourself Why."

Baldwin linked white people's evasion of death to their fear of sensuality.

Baldwin identified this white avoidance as a fundamental bypassing of the self and its impulses, especially sexual desire and fear. White delusional culture deemed low social status and sensuality to be sinful and immoral. They desired innocence, which they correlated with abstinence. As a result, Baldwin surmised, white people repressed their instinctive attraction to others. To circumvent their anxieties—to assuage a sense of inferiority and fear of being diminished or sinful, Baldwin argued—white people constructed a "nigger."

Throughout his life, Baldwin remained preoccupied with the question, *Why do they need a "nigger"?* Baldwin proposed that the concept and construct of the "nigger" fueled a false, deluded sense of white superiority. Constructing a "nigger" helped white people avoid their shame and self-doubts. Without the construct of the "nigger," Baldwin analyzed, white Americans would be forced to confront their inner lives, including all of the insecurities and self-loathing embedded in their psyches. In a 1963 essay, "We Can Change the Country," Baldwin argued:

> It is the American Republic—repeat, the American Republic—which created something which they called a 'nigger." They created it out of necessities of their own. The nature of the crisis is that I am not a "nigger"—I never was. I am a man. The question with which the country is confronted is this: Why do you need a "nigger" in the first place, and what are you going to do about him now that he's moved out of his place? Because I am not what you said I was. And if my place, as it turns out, is not my place, then you are not what you said you were, and where's your place? There has never been in this country a Negro problem. I have never been upset by the fact that I have a broad nose, big lips, and kinky hair. *You* got upset. And now you must ask yourself why.[33]

This was, for me, a poignant analysis. Baldwin was pointing to my grandparents and the conditions they had created in my young life. They were upset with my father's dark skin, broad nose, big lips, and kinky hair. They were repelled by *my* dark skin, broad nose, big lips, and kinky hair. Why? Reading Baldwin, I was struck by the fact that my father represented for them a sense of degradation. I, in turn, represented a defilement. I was the product of interracial sex. Moreover, I was the product of sex between a Black man who had moved out of his place, and a white woman who, in their eyes, had been polluted by Blackness.

They did not know what to do with their rage, their shame, except to project it onto me. But Baldwin made clear: This was not *my* problem. This was their problem. This was a white problem.

Projecting their shame onto Black people, Baldwin argued, was the only way that white Americans knew how to maintain their deluded sense of superiority. And they created conditions so that their white delusion would be the norm, the standard of purity. Baldwin posited that the only way to break through such ignorance was for white people to confront their fears. In a famous 1963 dialogue with Malcolm X,

Baldwin stated that "there was nothing sadder than a white man in the South who had nothing more than his skin and blue eyes and yellow hair."[34] For Baldwin, the emphasis on hair, eyes, and skin tone was extended to the spectacle of lynchings, whereby white men castrated Black men. White men were concerned with the elevated social status conveyed by their white bodies, as well as the threat posed by the idea of Black men's sexuality.

For Baldwin, self-doubt and shame were inextricably connected to white male fears of inferior sexual prowess and desirability. It was immeasurably easier to castrate the Black man than to confront these fears.

In short, whereas white American men sought to project strength and masculine power, Baldwin saw weakness and sexual insecurity. If white American men had sought to uplift Black men rather than degrade them, Baldwin thought, they would have embodied strength. But avoiding their insecurities led to unspeakable horrors for Black people, including lynching and castration. As a result, Baldwin said, he could not respect white myths of morality. He saw these projections for what they were: masks and lies that perpetuate white delusion.

It Comes from Somewhere

Baldwin, who never identified as Buddhist, was nevertheless the voice that helped me to embrace Buddhism as relevant to the particular experiences of Black people in the United States. Here was a way to cultivate practices of confronting fear and delusion. It felt more important than ever to acknowledge within my Buddhist practice that *yes*, it is the case that we suffer because we thirst. We suffer because we cling to stories and people that are impermanent. *And*, we suffer because we are entangled in a web of delusion and conditions that perpetuates harm. Parsing through the Buddhist doctrine of causes and conditions, guided by Baldwin's insights, helped me understand the task of acknowledging our conditions and the delusion that arises from them. It helped me to understand the white delusion that was embedded in my grandparents' psyches to such a degree that they denied the existence of their Black grandchildren. It helped me to contextualize the harm my father caused. I could hold in front of me this recognition: *The harm comes from somewhere.*

And yet. Even with white people's fear of death and sexuality ever present, Baldwin said, Black people garner stamina and unyielding presence. In spite of it all, Baldwin argued, Black people possess dignity, the capacity for emotional maturity. Those of us who can face death and the fear of sexuality learn to grow up.

I was devastated by my grandparents. Somehow, I felt differently about my father. He had suffered trauma over generations. I could understand his suffering, whereas I could not understand my maternal grandparents' shame. My father's transgressions had caused harm, and I lived with those wounds, daily. And yet, I had a greater sense of the psychological harm inflicted on him by the sheer violence of living as a Black man in America. In many ways, I shared his experiences.

I heard my father's suffering as I listened to Baldwin describe his youth. When he fled to France with $40 in his pocket, Baldwin had left conditions, similar to my father's, that overwhelmed him. In France he sought conditions in which he could feel the intensity of his suffering as a human, unrelentingly, without attempting to avoid or escape his suffering. It was only then that he started to heal.

But this inner work for Baldwin, and for me, is part of a larger commitment: changing the degrading conditions that lead to psychological despair. That political work, of taking on poverty and desperate housing conditions, of dismantling the system of mass incarceration, of creating access to living wage jobs, affordable housing, and health care—that work, too, is at the forefront of what it means to practice Buddhism. In changing our conditioning, collectively, we also seek to change conditions that lead to despair.

PRACTICE
N-RAIN

A powerful meditation for gaining perspective on the causes and conditions of suffering is a practice known as "RAIN." It has been evolved by dharma teachers in the Insight (Western Vipassana) tradition.[35] I have found RAIN to be especially useful working with deep grief over long periods of time.

RAIN stands for:

Recognition

Awareness

Investigation

Non-Attachment

RAIN practice typically starts when we recognize or name that which we are suffering. However, I have found it useful to start RAIN practice by first taking refuge—that is, by cultivating compassion for myself. Sometimes in RAIN practice, as I encounter grief and other deeply painful feelings, I have found the need to draw upon a wellspring of self-compassion to fully feel the anguish that arises.

Therefore, I refer to this practice as "N-RAIN."

Nurturing

Recognition

Awareness

Investigation

Non-Attachment

In the first step, Nurturing, you will practice cultivating a sense of being cared for. You may imagine a divine being who infuses you with a great sense of benevolence or bring to mind a person with whom you have or have had a supportive relationship. You may remember a time in which you were held tenderly. The energy that you are attempting to tap into is a broad energetic field: Knowing that you are loved.

If this first step is difficult, spend time wishing yourself well-being. The metta phrases "May I be safe and protected," "May I be peaceful and happy," "May I be healthy and strong," and "May I live with ease and well-being" serve as mantras to cultivate nurturing.

In the Recognition step of RAIN, you simply recognize that you are suffering. In this step, you may find it useful to simply say, "I am suffering" or "there is suffering right now." The most important part of this acknowledgment is the pause. Instead of reacting unconsciously to whatever is coming at you, you are gaining the capacity to recognize that you are suffering. You are cultivating the capacity to see the nuances of your suffering without seeking to fix it or take it away. Just being able to behold your suffering in the midst of it all is a momentous step toward being able to effectively work with it.

The Awareness step in RAIN is when you become aware that your suffering has causes and conditions, that it comes from somewhere. We are interconnected beings; we are always responding to people and conditions around us. You may become aware that your suffering shows up in particular ways, that it is a specific response to specific conditions. At this step, you may want to name the particular ways in which your suffering is arising, for example, as "grief" or "anger." You may seek to name the conditions and situations in which your suffering is arising. It is as though you are putting your suffering in the palm of your hand and examining its shape and texture, as well as its surrounding environment.

This process leads to Investigation of your suffering. You may ask yourself:

- What led to my suffering?

- Where does my suffering show up in my body?

- How does it show up?

Often we get wrapped up in narratives about why we suffer. But in meditation practice, the work is to transcend the narratives and simply show up for ourselves. The importance of Investigation is to notice details: Figure out what came before the experience of suffering and how it impacts you. You don't want to dismiss the conditions. You want to acknowledge them. You don't want to dismiss the ways in which your suffering manifests. You want to notice them.

The last step of RAIN is sometimes called Non-attachment and sometimes it is called Nurture. In Non-attachment, you recognize that your suffering is not personal. This is sometimes hard for people who have suffered deep harm to hear. The idea behind non-attachment is to not bond with your suffering. This is an important practice, but it can take years to internalize. If this teaching does not resonate for you, return to the practice of nurturing yourself. Wish yourself well-being and an end to your suffering. You have done the hard work of showing up for yourself; you can wish yourself compassion as you conclude your meditation.

Training Anger with Accuracy

Thus, it's the case that brave-hearted (bodhisattvas), like peacocks, transform into a nutriment the disturbing emotions—which are like the jungles of poison—and (thereby) engage themselves in the jungles of recurring samsara. In having gladly taken it on themselves, they're able to destroy this poison.

—DHARMARAKSITA, "WHEEL-WEAPON," VERSE 6

I spent decades circling around my grandparents' rejection, but it was my mother's own unresolved wounds and her self-interest that deepened the injury. My mother was a woman who took the blows handed down to her—in the form of her mother's daily beatings—well into adolescence. She was treated poorly by male partners throughout her early adult life. She had not learned how to stand up for herself, and she could not stand up for me.

She had children, she often told me, because she wanted to be loved.

Over her lifetime, my mother went through rebellious phases against her parents, first joining the anti–Vietnam War movement in the 1960s and then marrying a dark-skinned Puerto Rican poet. He was a member of the Young Lords, a political group in Chicago. In response, her parents disowned her, telling her that he was unacceptable because he did not look like Ricky Ricardo from *I Love Lucy*.

But these spurts of rebellion were superficial and short-lived. Until me. My existence could not be denied: I was embodied, a reminder of an on-and-off relationship that lasted nine years. I was born in 1975, a baby that, to my mother's parents, appeared in the world unexpectedly dark. They had not known about my father and thus did not anticipate my Black identity. They disowned my mother again.

By the time I was in the middle years of childhood, staring at the bulletin board in my grandparents' kitchen, I was grappling with rejection on numerous levels. My mother had moved on from her relationship with my father and had started dating a series of white men. A few years later, she married my stepfather, a conservative Christian. I was twelve and did not know what to make of this new dynamic in my home. It was a difficult period. And it got harder. A decade later, my grandparents planned their fiftieth wedding anniversary. They told my mother she could attend their celebration—but only without her Black children. She attended and left my thirteen-year-old brother at home. I was away at college. She did not tell me anything.

I found out about the celebration in passing, through another family member. It was a betrayal that lodged in my cells and in my bones; it radiated outward. My rage had no limits. It led to depressing, crushing fury and grief.

This anguish haunted me well into adulthood.

My mother did not stand up for me; she did not protect me or my brother. She did not tell my grandparents to go to hell. Years later, as I sat with my rage and my shame around her lack of protection, I came to understand yet another level of white delusion: self-protection at all costs. I have felt myself circling around my family's betrayal, attempting to navigate their myopia and respond in ways that allow parts of my sense of self to remain intact. For long periods of time, I have felt I have no roots, no origins. All I've had are my books—the voices of Black poets and writers who made a way out of no way. Artists who found a way forward while refusing to repress their pain.

I am aware that when I wrestle with my family dynamics, my rage is layered with grief. Heavy, weighted, the kind of grief in which I could drown. For many years, I was too alone, too young, forced to fight battles that were not mine. *Can I tend to my grief?* I've asked myself.

In public spaces, this anger shows up as fiery rage. I feel anger when my needs are disregarded—by administrators, for example. I am enraged when they exploit my labor and goodwill in the workplace and are not responsive to my salary needs. I experience racism in these interactions, time and again. I am angry with school officials who refuse to test my son for learning disabilities, even when his needs are very apparent, and it falls on me to figure out a way forward through the private education system. I am furious with federal employees who move the benchmarks when I am attempting to access relief aid after a natural disaster. Their dismissiveness and the sheer practical consequences of being denied set me off. This is valid rage. And if I am to move forward constructively and not just descend into anxiety and depression, I must train it with accuracy. This is when I turn to my practice. Here, I am not alone: I lean on James Baldwin, who named the love underneath his fury; I turn to Audre Lorde, who taught me about self-mothering amid internalized hatred and rage. Both of them showed me the importance of embracing anger and learning from it.

"Anger Is Loaded with Information and Energy"

Audre Lorde spoke of observing anger, parsing its dimensions. She noted: "It is not the anger of other women that will destroy us but our refusals to stand still, to listen to its rhythms, to learn within it, to move beyond the manner of presentation to the substance, to tap that anger as an important source of empowerment."[1] She and Baldwin identified anger as a useful emotion that is "loaded with information and energy."[2] For Lorde, anger was validated as that which illuminates an aspect of life that is out of alignment or simply wrong. She spoke of anger as a teacher, as an intensity that can transform us and our conditions. It provides agency, even dignity, if we do not allow it to destroy us. Other feminist writers as well speak of anger as a catalyst that is especially powerful when our rights and humanity are denied.[3]

Lorde described her anger in fiery terms: "a molten pond at the core of me," "a boiling hot spring likely to erupt at any point, leaping out of my consciousness like a fire on the landscape." In "Eye to Eye: Black Women, Hatred, and Anger," she elaborated:

> I know how much of my life as a powerful feeling woman is laced through with this net of rage. It is an electric thread woven into every emotional tapestry upon which I set the essentials of my life. . . . How to train that anger with accuracy rather than deny it has been one of the major tasks of my life.[4]

For Lorde, channeling anger was fundamentally creative work. Her rage gained traction in her poems; it fueled her commitment to the Black freedom movements and to the second-generation women's movement. It grounded her stamina as she fought for lesbian and gay visibility in majority-Black spaces and publishing projects. The oxygen Lorde gave to her anger shifted her energy from tending to the feelings of white women and Black men who centered themselves to the very-needed (but often less-acknowledged) work of elevating Black and lesbian women's experiences. She refused to participate in the dominant cultural patterns of marginalizing her own life, and the lives of other Black, queer people. Her anger, fierce and disruptive, would not allow her to self-silence. She wrote:

> Every woman has a well-stocked arsenal of anger potentially useful against those oppressions, personal and institutional, which brought that anger into being. Focused with precision it can become a powerful source of energy serving progress and change. And when I speak of change, I do not mean a simple

switch of positions or a temporary lessening of tensions, nor the ability to smile or feel good. I am speaking of a basic and radical alteration in those assumptions underlining our lives.[5]

She was talking about the hard work of holding activists in movement spaces accountable. Beyond platitudes, she demanded that white women within the women's movement take responsibility for their racism. She required that men within the Black freedom movement take responsibility for their sexism and homophobia. Change in society could only take place if movement activists realized it for themselves first.

What she sought, it seemed to me, required extraordinary internal capacity. It takes tremendous energy to work through conflict, especially with the pressures of work, and child and home care. But Lorde had all of those responsibilities, and she was still committed to the intensity of working through conflict within women's communities. If she was going to confront racism, patriarchy, and homophobia in Ronald Reagan's America, she was going to start with the people she called her own.

"If You Can't Look at It, You Can't Change It"

Anger was a generative force for Lorde as well as Baldwin, writes the philosopher Myisha Cherry.[6] She argues that for Baldwin, anger arises from an "examined life."[7] It is not simply a knee-jerk, impulsive reaction, but rather, a thoughtful and intentional responsiveness. In turning toward anger and acknowledging how it manifested in his body as a result of personal and systemic injustice, Baldwin validated Black rage. He was conscious of its origins and aware of its manifestations. It was embodied and epistemic. Like others who feel Black rage, Baldwin took apart the myths and masks endemic to white America and refused to participate in its myopic rituals. He was angry at America's unwillingness to confront its superficial lies.

Baldwin saw first the rage within himself. In his essay "Notes of a Native Son," he described his rage as an unrelenting sickness that gripped his body when he was denied service at a restaurant in Princeton, New Jersey.

> Once this disease is contracted, one can never be really care-free again, for the fever, without an instant's warning, can recur at any moment. . . . There is not a Negro alive who does not have this rage in his blood—one has the choice, merely, of living with it consciously and surrendering to it. As for me, this fever has recurred in me, and does, and will until the day I die.[8]

The rage shows up as heat. It takes over the body. But Baldwin did not attempt to make it go away: Baldwin's "pounding in the skull and fire in the bowels" are valid. Moral. Justified. And yet, Baldwin was clear that intimacy with rage on its own, without examination, is fruitless. He saw this futile, bitter rage in his stepfather's psyche, and he refused to let it take over his own.

Baldwin claimed that just rage was a force for social change. He validated the wrath of Huey P. Newton and the Black Panther Party, the fury of Angela Y. Davis and Maya Angelou, the bitterness of Elijah Muhammad, Malcolm X, and the Nation of Islam. These were fierce activists who turned toward the poison of anger and metabolized it by forming community organizations that uplifted Black dignity and agency.

Baldwin, through art, metabolized his own fury. Using the blues as a guide, he embraced anger as a source of love. He felt the possibility of transformation while listening to the blues, music that evoked a depth of love, directed first at oneself and simultaneously at one's people. In his short story "Sonny's Blues," Baldwin reflected, Black music was an expression of Black rage and pain, and, at the same time, a source of soothing, of self-actualization. The blues evoke timeless suffering—ruin and destruction, despair and death. We, as listeners, are asked to show up in the present, to find a path of joy amid the trauma. In playing and singing the blues, Baldwin argued, Black people can speak for themselves and we, the listeners, can be free. But we must listen carefully. And the blues musicians themselves can also be liberated—but only if we would listen to *them*.[9] We need each other, the character Creole in Baldwin's "Sonny's Blues" explained. Creole "was Sonny's witness that deep water and drowning were not the same thing—he had been there, and he knew."[10]

Like Lorde, Baldwin was preoccupied with agency: the ability to seize responsibility for one's existence, despite navigating the atrocities enacted upon Black Americans. This required looking at his suffering directly. Cherry sums up Baldwin's approach: "If you don't look at it, you can't change it."[11]

And, Baldwin emphasized, it is important to look at Black suffering with compassion. Baldwin was sympathetic to Black figures who expressed murderous bitterness. He evoked empathy in his second play, *Blues for Mister Charlie*, which he acknowledged in the introduction was based on the 1955 murder of Emmett Till in Mississippi. The play ends on a note of resignation and despair.[12] So, too, does Baldwin's novel *If Beale Street Could Talk*, a story of a Northern couple that is in love but forced to contend with racism and the brutality of the penal system.[13] The characters are drawn with a depth of empathy as they navigate violent, corrupt institutions.

Baldwin further displayed compassion for Black characters created by fellow Black writers. He reflected on his response to Richard Wright's *Native Son*, seeing in the character of Bigger a Black man who is the product of the poverty and violence endemic to Chicago slums. He empathized with Wright's frustration even as he ultimately disavowed Wright's final message of inevitable violence and moral pathology on the part of Black people. In Baldwin's eyes, Black people *can* still love themselves and one another, despite the degrading conditions to which they are subjected. In reflecting on Baldwin, Cherry observes:

> Black folk, like any other moral agent, can deliberate and act, make it useful to value others, protest conditions, and ultimately change the world. This ability to choose [is what] Baldwin calls our attention to. He highlights how Black agency is revealed both in Black people's ability to not be controlled by anger, as well as to choose what their anger will do in the world. Black rage is not just something that Black folk can *feel*, it is also a way to act in the world. Black rage is a way to respond to the world in a critical, loving, and creative way, all in the service of dismantling the racial causes and conditions for it. And in doing so, Baldwin not only defends emotion, but also Black life, and Black people's moral and political possibilities.[14]

The love underlying Baldwin's rage is simultaneously a compassion that cuts through delusion and conditioning. Just the process of acknowledging anger, even murderous rage, is a practice of claiming one's own agency. He would rather swallow the poison of anger than live a life of deception, Baldwin decided. He did not want to succumb to the myopia embedded in white institutions that are content to murder hundreds of thousands of Black people while the white citizens upholding those institutions *do not want to know* that they are participating in annihilation.

He was compelled to swallow the poison not only for his own healing, but for all Black people who are subjected to the hatred embedded in white supremacy. And, for a time, he had hope that "relatively conscious" Black and white people collectively could transform racism in America.

"A Practice of Non-Reactivity"

It took time for me to internalize Baldwin's optimistic message of agency.

The rage that Baldwin described, the "dread disease," was inflamed at any experience of disregard I had. *I worked so hard*, I'd think when I was dismissed. When I extended myself generously and was taken for granted by white supervisors, I was *angry*. When I was lied to and publicly undermined, I was enraged. The persistent patterns of extraction and exploitation at the hands of administrators drove me to a place of fury, time and again. I was constantly cleaning up other people's messes—bridges they had burned, projects that they had not finished, promises that they had not kept. But even after I had extended myself, they did not value me; they only wanted more. As had been the case with my mother and her parents, they saw me as existing to serve them. In their eyes, I did not have needs. I was there to be used. And when I articulated my boundaries or acknowledged the patterns of extraction, they suggested that they could easily replace me.

Yes, I was angry. But what could I do with my rage? In my twenties, I did not know how to deal with my own "boiling hot spring [which was] likely to erupt at any point."[15] It was easier to submerge it and keep going. But inevitably the repressed anger turned into depression and anxiety. This is when I embraced Buddhist practice. As I began to learn the teachings and to meditate, I was able to cultivate spaciousness around my rage, to acknowledge it and let it breathe. I let myself explore its texture, to discover it to be hard or soft, to give it a color and sometimes a face. I let myself roar like a lion, in private, when I needed to, sometimes while running or driving. I referred to these practices as giving my rage oxygen. The practice of exhaling my anger, rather than repressing it or acting out of it, was a practice of metabolizing. In solitude, I let my body process intense anger on its own terms.

In the presence of other people, I was careful, more restrained. I was afraid of harming others with my intensity, and consequently of being exiled, cut off. I was afraid of committing damage that I could not repair. Here, I practiced with anger by cultivating non-reactivity and the capacity to pause. Buddhist teachers helped me to find inner stability in the midst of confusion and rage. They helped me to stop participating in my own oppression. I could take refuge, again and again, in my own person. These practices helped me to identify a place of safety within my body—my belly or my chest—and become deeply attuned to it. By paying attention to the rise and fall of my breath, I created a sense of emotional stability.

Cultivating the capacity to take refuge in my body was a turning point in my practice. I finally had a place for the raw anger to land. But it was a fine line between not reacting and repressing my anger— that is, self-silencing. Even if I cultivated inner refuge, I still needed to be in relationship with other people—including the people who had created harm. I looked to Audre Lorde as someone who had learned to speak her anger, to tell white women what it felt like to be used as a service for their own emotional processing. Lorde was direct. She was vocal when she felt used. I needed these muscles, I realized. In each situation, I still had to make choices. I still had to *act*. I honored my anger by leaving toxic situations, especially when I realized just how much emotional labor I expended when I was pre-paring to engage with exploitative administrators and nonresponsive bureaucrats.

But there were times when it was not an option to leave. And I did not always want to give up on interpersonal relationships. Over time, when I felt harmed by friends and family members, I was able to take refuge and then repair with them. That was a big step for me. I tried in each case to understand their context, to ask where they were coming from. I tried to speak directly when the situation called for it. I learned to establish boundaries. I leaned into my Buddhist practice to discern a way forward.

Anger in Vajrayana Buddhism

What I learned from Vajrayana Buddhism, after many years of sitting practice, was to validate my rage and see its energy as fuel. This was not anathema to Buddhism, as I had thought during my initial venture into the tradition. Early Buddhism and forms of Mahayana Buddhism (the second "turning of the wheel") describe anger as a defilement, a poison. In these lineages, anger is a negative state of mind; it impedes liberation. But this can be problematic. Repressed anger, masquerading as calm, can be misconstrued as tolerance of extractive behavior, allowing other people to take advantage of me and others who were exploited.

Vajrayana Buddhism spoke of turning poisons into the energy required for liberation. I appreciated the teachings of the Indian Buddhist guru Dharmaraksita on the usefulness of anger. How might it be metabolized so that its energy could fuel change in the most generative ways?

In the ninth or tenth century, the Indian Buddhist Dharmaraksita orally transmitted teachings to his student, Atisha. Dharmaraksita taught that bodhisattvas—enlightened beings who choose to stay on earth and help guide humans through suffering—are like peacocks roaming a bountiful garden. The beautiful birds have many medicinal plants at their disposal, but rather than choosing healing herbs, the peacocks intentionally seek out poisonous stalks and swallow them. In so doing, they metabolize and transform the plants' poison and transform it into edification. The brave-hearted peacocks (bodhisattvas) thereby demonstrate how to work effectively with intense, complex emotions—even feelings as overwhelming as rage—by embracing those feelings with skill. In so doing, the peacocks transform these afflictive emotions, using them for growth and service.

Such metabolization requires rigorous training, Dharmaraksita taught. He instructed students of the dharma to focus on harnessing the power of afflictive emotions through mental practices. He was primarily intent upon transforming anger for the purpose of personal, moral, and spiritual development.

In my eyes, Dharmaraksita anticipated James Baldwin and Audre Lorde. His teaching showed me a way to work effectively with intense, complex anger. It involved action: turning toward. Not repressing. Not dismissing. Not ignoring. Seeking out. Acknowledging. Seeing the poison, in all of its potential wildness, in all of its potential healing. There are several steps to this practice: It is not just seeing the poison and accepting it. It is swallowing it, internalizing it. This practice involves stillness and movement, all at once.

Metabolizing rage in Buddhist practice fostered my understanding of Baldwin and Lorde as spiritual ancestors who had paved a way out of no way. Baldwin and Lorde, too, spoke of the usefulness of anger. Rather than avoiding rage, I could follow in the footsteps of Baldwin and Lorde. I could be like the peacock, swallow the poison, use it as edification. Anger could be a seed for transformation.

I could *do* something with my rage at being exploited. I could see it. I could validate it. I could let it move through my body and fuel my commitments, to myself and others. I could train it with accuracy.

"A Powerful Source of Energy Serving Progress and Change"

It was not easy to channel this fire at first. Anger is hard to bear, Lorde acknowledged. Women, for one, have inherited distorted ways of thinking and relating, but seeing the ways in which women's power has been used against us can also be a source of strength. The insights that arise from recognizing and examining anger are inherently transformative. Lorde wrote: "For anger between peers births change, not destruction, and the discomfort and sense of loss it often causes is not fatal, but a sign of growth."[16]

Lorde's words foretell the analysis of the Buddhist psychologist Anita Barrows, who writes that anger is "a deep wellspring of strength and positive force for many kinds of change." Rather than "correcting" anger, Barrows says, human beings can develop skillful means to work with it. They can access, rather than lose touch with, their anger.[17]

Barrows asks:

Rather than using our practice to boil down our anger, why can't we use it to explore it, to honor it, to give it amplitude, to restore its vitality, its usefulness, its freedom from destructiveness? Can we imagine that such anger, fully experienced, can initiate a process leading to the envisioning of possibility? Such anger would be replete with authority, grace, confidence. It would not be petty. It would embrace complexity and be channeled compassionately, but it would not resist the setting of limits, the standing firm, the necessary delineation of boundaries. Its aim would not be vengeance, punishment, humiliation . . . its aim would not be to continue the cycle of suffering, but rather to interrupt it and establish something new in its stead. It would not get stuck in victimization, bitterness, resentment, obsessive rumination on the wound. It would not be equated with aggression, which seeks power over the other. Because it would be expressed openly, wholesomely, it would not do its work by manipulation or deceit.[18]

Barrows is pointing to the possibilities of learning from anger rather than defaulting to a pattern of repressing it. So, too, did Lorde. What stunts growth, Lorde argued, is attempting to subdue anger. "My response to racism is anger," Lorde wrote. "That anger has eaten clefts into my living only when it remained unspoken, useless to anyone."[19] Vajrayana Buddhist gurus said this as well. Repressed anger cannot be used; that is, it cannot be fuel. Anger needs oxygen to be metabolized and transformed; only then can it be a source of power.

I loved how Lorde sought to know the nuances of anger. I was in awe of her capacity to articulate her rage publicly, rather than smothering it. She expressed it most starkly, it seemed to me, in her interactions with white women in the second-generation feminist movement, with whom she insisted on acknowledging the manifestations of racism and other social differences.

Refusing Distortions

Lorde's theory of difference is a powerful testament to her personal sense of authority. She refused to adapt to the norms of the dominant white, male, patriarchal culture; so too she refused to collapse women's experiences under the label of "woman," as this term assumes a white woman's norm. She redefined power above and beyond the parameters that were given as a "mythical norm." Power, for Lorde, was not appearing as "white, thin, male, young, heterosexual, christian [sic], and financially secure."[20] Rather, power arose in the process of identifying and embracing differences.

Lorde argued that white women should recognize differences among community members and refuse conventional definitions of "woman," "lesbian," "mother," and "Black." She stated:

By and large within the women's movement today, white women focus upon their oppression as women and ignore differences of race, sexual preference, class, and age. There is a pretense to a homogeneity of experience covered by the word *sisterhood* that does not in fact exist.[21]

Confronting dominant white male power—the "primary oppressor"[22]—requires a woman-centered movement, Lorde argued. Yet she expressed rage at the assumptions made by white women. She refused to gloss over the varied social realities of women of color, impoverished women, immigrant women, and mothers, even as many white women suggested that all female-bodied people share similar oppression. The concerns of white women and Black women are not the same, Lorde wrote. "You [white women] fear your children will grow up to join the patriarchy and testify against you, we [Black women] fear our children will be dragged from a car and shot down in the street, and you will turn your backs upon the reasons they are dying."[23]

She pointed to exploitative dynamics among different races and classes of women, critiquing the extractive nature of white women who "use the maternal labor of Black women as domestic servants to buy their own freedom."[24] Lorde noted that there was, in the experience of exploitation, an isolation that Black women experienced: Their very lives were marginalized and extracted from by their "sisters." This experience naturally bred valid anger. And still, this anger could be useful if women acknowledged the differences between them.

Over decades of activism in the feminist movement, Lorde called out ways in which white women maintain their racial privilege.

> In order to recognize that racism is a feminist issue it requires being able to see that racism, sexism, homophobia, elitism, ageism have their root in the same inability to accept difference in a structure that depends on profit for its survival. That society is so highly structured that those on the bottom then generate energy and power, and that power is used by the people on top. If you *believe* that you are towards the top, you are very terrified of being dropped down below. It is essentially divide and conquer.[25]

In this way, Lorde indicted white women for the way in which they participate in institutional and cultural oppression. She was often angry as she did so. Anger served as fuel, an energy that expanded when she refused to ignore harm. "Anger is an appropriate reaction to racist attitudes, as is fury when the actions arising from those attitudes do not change," she stated. She encouraged white women to work through their fear of anger and prioritize honest examination of themselves, for, she argued, the desire to settle for superficial solidarity would crumble beneath the weight of hatred leveled upon women by white, patriarchal, homophobic institutions.[26]

She felt like "fire in the ice zone of uncomprehending eyes of white women," when she observed white women's self-interest—their fear and guilt—which rendered them unable to acknowledge Black women's realities. When Black women bring anger to the surface and channel it into difficult situations, Lorde said, it becomes "a powerful source of energy serving progress and change."[27]

Lorde validated anger as a source of energy on multiple fronts. Even as she indicted white feminist communities for their racism, she challenged the cultures of Black freedom movements, which were dominated by Black men who often shunned lesbian and gay-identified activists and reiterated homophobic narratives replete in the white world. In Black movement spaces, Lorde sought to expand the definitions of freedom by confronting anti-gay attitudes and patriarchy.

She periodically found herself on the margins in Black art and political spaces, as prominent Black men and women identified Lorde as "dangerous and suspect."[28] But she refused to acquiesce to the idea of monolithic Blackness within the Black freedom movement. "The need for unity is often misnamed as a need for homogeneity and a Black feminist vision mistaken for betrayal of our common interests as a people," she wrote.[29] She referred to homophobia in the Black freedom movement as "sexual hostility" that functioned like a disease, arguing that avoidance bolstered illness rather than healing it.

Lorde directly named physical violence by Black men against Black women as a result of powerlessness experienced by Black men. She theorized that Black men seek to take the place of white men, thus inhabiting a socially powerful position. In an interview reflecting upon her relationship with her father, a proud Black Caribbean man, she identified herself as his enemy.[30] As a Black lesbian who refused to be closeted in Black movement spaces, Lorde intuited that she posed a psychological threat to Black men's desire for white male power. She found herself ostracized in Black literary circles.

And it was not only Black men who were threatened by her lesbian identity. Lorde experienced a corresponding isolation among sister Black women. She refused an "easy blackness."[31] In her biomythography *Zami: A New Spelling of My Name* she recounted an experience of opening a locker at work and feeling fury when a hair-straightening comb tumbled out.[32] By wearing her hair naturally, rather than processing it, Lorde had transgressed dominant cultural habits among Black women who straightened their hair. But she refused to suppress her curls. The body speaks its own history, Lorde insisted.[33] She embraced her body, including her hair, as authentic. She rejected processed hair as a representation of internalized racism. Her refusal to pander to whiteness extended to other modes of self-expression as well. She sought to root herself in African traditions, including celebrating African deities and wearing colorful West African garb.

Lorde's embrace of unconventional cultural norms, and her expansive, unrepressed fury, resulted in persistent isolation and intermittent desolation in movement spaces. She was often sad. And angry. "It was hard enough to be Black, to be Black and female, to be Black, female, and gay. To be Black, female, and gay, and out of the closet in a white environment, even to the extent of dancing in the Bagatelle, was considered by many Black lesbians to be simply suicidal."[34] According to Lorde's biographer Alexis De Veaux, Lorde's poem, "Between Ourselves," "signaled a willingness to forego the black community's elusive embrace, though not the black liberation struggle, for a more complex accounting of its history and her own."[35] Lorde further confronted the idea of monolithic Blackness in her essay "Age, Race, Class and Sex: Women Defining Difference":

> Differences among ourselves as Black women are also being misnamed and used to separate us from one another. As a Black lesbian feminist comfortable with the many different ingredients of my identity, and a woman committed to racial and sexual freedom from oppression, I find I am constantly being encouraged to pluck out one aspect of myself and present this as the meaningful whole, eclipsing or denying the other parts of self. But this is a destructive and fragmenting way to live. My fullest concentration of energy is available to me only when I integrate all the parts of who I am, openly, allowing power from particular sources of my living to flow back and forth freely through all my different selves, without the restrictions of externally

imposed definition. Only then can I bring myself and my energies as a whole to the service of those struggles which I embrace
as part of my living.[36]

Lorde sought to liberate all persons whose marginalization within
the mainstream white social order fueled their resistance to domination. Those who are oppressed must acknowledge, indeed, *use,* different aspects of their experiences and identity in the service of political
and cultural liberation. If we do not, Lorde argued, we will turn the
anger we feel toward oppressors against one another. During the sole
public conversation between Lorde and Baldwin, which took place in
1984 at Hampshire College in Amherst, Massachusetts, the two luminaries debated that point.[37] Lorde reiterated that distinctions among
women and experiences of sexism in the Black community must be
acknowledged and constructively addressed.

At the same time, Lorde distinguished anger from hatred. Anger
must be known and trained in order to serve as fuel for a way forward.
Anger, for her, was useful but "limited." It clarified the past; it fostered
scrutiny and insight into the devastation that landed upon Black wom-
en's bodies and psyches. It supported and enabled Black women's fortitude. And yet, Lorde said, anger alone cannot create the future; it
does not, on its own, naturally evolve into tenderness. Moreover, it is
close to hatred, which can corrode a person. Anger needs to be tended
to with love. Baldwin thought the same.

"Anger, Used, Does Not Destroy"

Anger is a bell, a signal of injustice. And yet. It is often the result of
experiencing hatred. Baldwin viewed hatred as a state of mind that can
destroy a person. He watched hatred consume his stepfather, and he
felt the seeds of hatred within himself. Remembering his experience of
discrimination in the American Diner in Princeton, New Jersey, Baldwin wrote, "I saw nothing very clearly, but I did see this: that my life,

real life, was in danger, and not from anything other people might do but from the hatred I carried in my own heart."[38]

Baldwin envisioned his stepfather

sitting at the window, locked up in his terrors; hating and fearing every living soul including his children who had betrayed him, too, by reaching toward the world which had despised him.[39]

Baldwin further reflected:

He had lived and died in an intolerable bitterness of spirit and it frightened me, as we drove him to the graveyard through those unquiet, ruined streets, to see how powerful and overflowing this bitterness could be and to realize that this bitterness was now mine.[40]

Hatred and fear are forms of an affliction, a state of mind that can destroy the self and that can, in turn, destroy others. Baldwin saw this capacity in himself. He also saw it in white people.

Hatred, Baldwin surmised, unconsciously drives the collective white psyche to oppress Black people in America. White America's hatred and fear of Black people result in conditions that inevitably devastate the Black mind and body. What follows is internalized hatred, a condition that Baldwin was determined to see and address directly.

I wanted to see this internalized hatred in myself, too. I had absorbed my white grandparents' hatred of me, my mother's betrayal, my father's abandonment, at an early age. In my adolescence and early twenties, I had moved in cycles of fear and self-loathing, like a hamster cycling in a wheel, unable to escape the misery of my conditioned mind. It was this perpetual sense of being stuck, caught in my terror and bitterness, that drove me to Buddhist practice. I had tried everything else, but nothing had alleviated the heaviness of internalized contempt.

It was incumbent upon me to parse through the weight of my emotions, to see their origins, to validate their existence. Anger at my grandparents' rejection of me, at my mother's betrayal of me, was just. Anger at exploitative administrators was valid. But the resultant bitterness was mine to bear. I could carry it, or I could find ways to metabolize it.

In a later essay—one of the two that Lorde described as being most important in her canon—Lorde elaborated her definitions of anger and hatred: "Anger [is] a passion of displeasure that may be excessive or misplaced but not necessarily harmful. Hatred—an emotional habit or attitude of mind in which aversion is coupled with ill will. Anger, used, does not destroy. Hatred does."[41]

In this pivotal essay "Eye to Eye: Black Women, Hatred, and Anger," Lorde wrote about her process of scrutinizing anger and her observation of a society in which "the deepest understructure . . . was hatred, that societal deathwish directed against us from the moment we were born Black and female in America."[42] The hatred emanating from a white woman on a subway train. The dismissiveness of an eye doctor who disparaged Lorde's intelligence. The derogatory treatment in a restaurant, in which her white friend was given water in a glass, and Lorde was given a paper cup. The denigrating images of Black children in books.

As the darkest-skinned child, who was also "bad, always in trouble," Lorde internalized that *bad* meant *Black*. This message was directed at her from the Black women to whom she was in closest proximity, the ones from whom she sought love and affection. Lorde reflected:

> From that moment [of being born Black and female in America] we have been steeped in hatred—for our color, for our sex, for our effrontery in daring to presume we had any right to live. As children we absorbed that hatred, passed it through ourselves, and for the most part, we still live our lives outside of the recognition of what that hatred really is and how it functions. Echoes of it return as cruelty and anger in our dealings with each other. For each of us bears the face that hatred seeks, and we have each learned to be at home with cruelty because we have survived so much of it within our own lives.[43]

By extension, Lorde was saying that, this hatred—unconsciously internalized from childhood interactions—manifests in anger toward Black women in adult life.

Lorde posited that all Black women—individually and collectively, *because they are Black women*—have absorbed virulent hatred. She celebrated Black women's capacity to endure the hatred. But she also recognized its costs and consequences.

The manifestations of that hatred, lacking scrutiny of its origins and skillful practices to care for it usefully, corrupt and unleash unbridled anger toward sister Black women. Thus, Lorde said, Black women "breed harshness and cruelty" with one another "where we most need softness and understanding."[44] In "Eye to Eye," she articulated dimensions of Black women's relationships.

> The language by which we have been taught to dismiss ourself and our feelings as suspect is the same language we use to dismiss and suspect each other. Too pretty—too ugly. Too Black—too white. Wrong. . . . We refuse to give up the artificial distances between us, or to examine our real differences for creative exchange. . . . We have not been allowed to experience each other freely as Black women in america; we come to each other coated in myths, stereotypes, and expectations from the outside, definitions not our own. . . . How are you judging me? As Black as you? Blacker than you? Not Black enough? Whichever, I am going to be found wanting in some way.[45]

Black women do not attempt to speak these painful truths with each other, Lorde went on. Moreover, Black women could be directly, intentionally cruel to one another. One reason for this, she surmised, is that Black women were not allowed to have childhoods; they could not "play at living" when they were young.[46] The stakes for survival were too high. She recalled the four Black girls killed in the church bombing during the civil rights movement. Hatred came at Black girls, violently. Just staying alive was hard.

There was political work to be done, Lorde said, to change those conditions from mere survival to conditions in which Black girls and women could thrive. But the first step of that political work was internal: honoring and embracing feelings.

The way forward, for Lorde, is in maternal care—of oneself first, and then, by extension, of sister Black women.

"We Will Begin to See Each Other"

Audre Lorde's complicated relationship with Black women was something I could relate to. As a young girl growing up on the northwest side of Chicago, I navigated starkly separate Black and white worlds with very little guidance from adults in my life. In most of my elementary schools—a different one every year—I was the only Black girl in my class. White students would stick pencils in my curls to see if they would fall out. I was supremely self-conscious of my dark skin and "nappy" hair, of how my body marked me as different.

And yet, I did not find greater ease with Black children. I spoke "proper" and was mocked for being too white. My hair, in particular, seemed to be a lightning rod. It garnered an exceptional amount of attention. Whereas white children made fun of my tight curls, Black children called my hair "good hair." It was the subject of catcalling from boys and jealousy from girls. We were all circling around an internalized white beauty standard, but it was hard to know it then. In high school, while I was working at a movie theater, another Black female worker told me with contempt: "You're not Nubian Black like the rest of us." In the same way that I had internalized white hatred, I let those words sink in. I seemed to have no buffer. I was angry. But I felt apologetic, too, like I had done something wrong. This was the dynamic to which Lorde was pointing. As Black women, we often went for each other's throats, weaponizing differences among each other. I appreciated that she could name it.

Like Lorde, I hungered for connection with Black girls and, later, Black women. I sought to belong, attain the "Black Card" that seemed so elusive, that would give me membership in the club. The patterns of exclusion, from white and Black children, would follow me for decades, like a shadow, like a war. In this way, too, I resonated with Lorde's pain. When I was interested in joining a Black sorority my first semester of college, I publicly asked a question about interracial dating. It was the wrong thing to say. There was cold silence in response.

I continued to ask awkward questions, always from the periphery. But I also self-silenced. Asking "wrong" questions demarcated me as a "Sister Outsider." A professor once told me flatly: "You don't know the cultural cues." I was hurt. Again, I let the words sink in. They stayed in the quicksand of my woundedness, my shame. Perhaps that professor did not know how much that comment hurt. But it reaffirmed a feeling that I had experienced from an early age.

In my late twenties, I was so isolated that once, when a Black woman stopped me in the street and spoke to me in a friendly tone, I was surprised. I remember registering my delight during the meditation practice that I had just started. My sense of exclusion was so heightened that I had nowhere to turn but inward; it was in taking refuge that I began to heal my wounds.

I needed safety. I needed mirroring. And within that context, I needed to befriend myself, become intimate with my suffering, my anger, my experience of being hated and the ways in which I had internalized that hatred. I looked to Audre Lorde as a guide.

"Mothering Ourselves"

Lorde advocated "mothering ourselves." For Lorde—who gave birth to two children—maternal love is first and foremost generative self-love. This self-love, in turn, organically extends out toward other Black women. Even when she felt wounded by sister Black women, Lorde continued to hunger for connection. In the relationships she culti-vated, she related to other women "in one of two ways, either as lover or as mother."[47] This maternal dynamic contrasted with the difficult relationship she had had with her biological mother, whom she expe-rienced as controlling and abusive. To mother others was a practice of healing the sense of alienation and disconnection she felt in her childhood. To mother herself with a depth of tenderness was a starting point for healing internalized hatred.

Lorde's practice of self-mothering fundamentally rested upon self-scrutiny, allowing feelings that were painful and chaotic to be inti-mately known. In "Eye to Eye," she wrote:

> We will begin to see each other as we dare to begin to see our-selves; we will begin to see ourselves as we begin to see each other, without aggrandizement or dismissal or recriminations, but with patience and understanding. . . . Mothering. Claiming some power over who we choose to be, and knowing that such power is relative within the realities of our lives. Yet knowing that only through the use of that power can we effectively change those realities.[48]

She continued: "I have to learn to love myself before I can love you or accept your loving. You have to learn to love yourself before you can love me or accept my loving."[49]

In her cultivation of a practice of deep self-nurturing, Lorde helped me to see the possibility of self-intimacy and self-compassion. This was a way forward. I understood her message in my bones. I had attempted to prac-tice in different Buddhist lineages until I found one that centered compas-sion practices. These rituals spoke to my yearning for maternal softness.

I heard from both Lorde and the Buddhist tradition: The practice of clearly seeing and embracing our own suffering can only be effective if we give ourselves the tenderness and affection that we often desper-ately want from our mothers.

I felt that Lorde's capacity to self-reflect and state, "When I can recognize my own worth, I can recognize yours," mirrored the metta practices of the Early Buddhist lineages: offering compassion to herself as well as other beings. The *Metta Sutta* speaks of maternal love as a bodhisattva warrior energy:

Even as a mother protects with her life
Her only child,
So with a boundless heart
Should one cherish all beings.[50]

Lorde made clear that cultivating maternal self-compassion fosters inner spaciousness. It is possible to navigate the world as a Black woman who has suffered harm, and to open into an experience of emptiness and fearlessness. Compassion and tenderness can soothe internalized hatred. In Lorde's practice of self-mothering, intimately knowing internalized hatred and anger made room for new ways of looking at herself and others.

The practice that Lorde invited Black women into is a practice of self-compassion. We start with ourselves, and our self-compassion radiates outward. By self-mothering, Black women can then extend compassion naturally to other Black women and be in solidarity with them. This way of being is akin to the Buddhist teaching on wisdom and skillful means.[51] Lorde was asking *and answering* questions that I had pursued my whole life: How can Black women acknowledge internalized self-hatred and heal it? How can Black women investigate our anger and recognize the ways in which they express it toward those persons in closest proximity to them? How can Black women cultivate compassion and wisdom? Audre Lorde answered these questions by pointing to tender self-mothering.

Ultimately, Audre Lorde's story of healing through self-mothering was also my own. I learned how to practice her wisdom with Black Buddhist teachers. It was not a paradox to realize that only when I cultivated mother-love in my own being could I befriend and deeply connect with other Black women.

The Practice of Metta

The practice of metta allowed me to feel the waves of rage cascade over me like the molten lava Lorde spoke of in her essay "Eye to Eye." And so much sadness. I had known the experience of hatred directed toward me, intimately. I attempted each day to breathe through the hatred and my fear of it, to parse through my anger, to give it oxygen. Sometimes I felt that, instead, I was drowning.

That was the practice: showing up for my anger, and all of the other feelings that circled around it, day after day. It was the practice of saying: *Yes, Anger, I see you. Yes, Grief, you are here, and I feel your intensity.* I learned to greet my rage and anguish and embrace it all, rather than shutting down and fleeing from the intensity of my pain. Many days, I just cried. My body needed release. Too much harm had become trapped, immobilized, in my cells. I needed to exhale, to let the tears come.

In establishing a daily practice, I was the peacock eating poison. I was a bird, beautiful and unable to fly, choosing poison that, *because I* decided to swallow it, nourished me. Had I chosen to avoid it, the poison would have caused me harm. But I embraced it. The act of embracing rather than repressing created just enough space for me to see myself with compassion, and to see my mother's wounds as well.

Compassion and clear seeing—sometimes referred to as two wings of a bird in Buddhist lineages—became my core practice. I could see the dynamics at work with my mother. I could work skillfully with my rage toward inept administrators. I could take on atrocities in the world around me and acknowledge: They come from somewhere. I could know that my rage is a valid, responsive, fury. Sometimes, it is still too much to hold. But through the practice of honoring all that arises, I can validate anger as a moral response to harm, as an outrage rooted in self-love and love for others.

Like Lorde and Baldwin, I have sought to transform my anger and make it personally useful. But it is more than beneficial just to me. My metabolized anger is also meant to be fuel for my people. I can feel my fury when Black people are gunned down by police officers in the US, when affordable housing and living-wage jobs disappear. I can feel my outrage when Palestinians in Gaza are trapped, bombed, displaced, and starved. It is moral, just anger. Like Baldwin and Lorde, like the peacock in Dharmaraksita's story, I validate my rage. Baldwin and Lorde were always guided by a greater purpose than their own moral and spiritual development. They were committed to social change. They wrote from their self-love and their love of Black people. And they transformed poison into power.

PRACTICE
Compassion for Ourselves

The following compassion practice became my daily practice while I researched and wrote a book on Black Buddhists in 2019. I gave myself permission to practice for long periods while I steeped myself in the voices of Black Buddhists. Ruth King's *Mindful of Race* is primarily focused on providing practical ways to heal (individually and as a society) from racism.[52] Racism is a heart disease, she writes, and we can heal it. The compassion practice she offers as part of this healing has been deeply grounding because she first instructs us as practitioners to invite in other beings who wish wellness for us. She invites us to connect to the earth. And she invites us to imagine that other beings who have our back are breathing with us.

GUIDED MEDITATION FROM RUTH KING

To begin, take a position of relaxed awareness and begin to connect with your own body and the larger body—earth—holding you. Bring awareness to the breath moving through your body, entering and exiting as the breath joins with the larger element air—air moving in, air moving through, air moving out. Take a few moments to rest and savor the presence of the earth and air—always with you.

Next, invite a trio of protection to surround you. You might imagine a bene-factor sitting right behind you—someone who is there for you with wise guidance. On the right of you is someone you deeply care for; and on your left is a younger, more innocent version of yourself. Imagine them sitting close enough for you to feel their warmth and care, as if their presence were wrapping you in a warm blanket. Allow every cell in your body to be bathed by this compassionate regard as you thank them for being with you. Feel the warmth from the earth and the mutual regard flowing between the four of you.

Take time to linger and rest in this initial practice. Stay present to your body and breath as you offer this compassion first to yourself, then to a challenging person or situation, and finally to all beings.

Bring to mind an aspect of yourself that needs your compassion. Maybe a part of you that has been suffering directly or that has been impacted by racial harm. Allow it to reveal itself naturally. This aspect of yourself may be clear or vague, younger or older, past or present—it does not matter. Gently invite it to come close, to sit before you, and to join your trio of protection.

Allow yourself to be touched by its presence. Welcome it, saying, "I care, I care," and ask it to tell you its story. For example, it may want to tell you how and why it feels ashamed, enraged, numb, lonely, abandoned, clueless, in hiding, sad, anxious, indifferent, wounded, determined, punishing, weary, or afraid. Listen with your entire body as you feel the support of Mother Earth beneath you and your trio of protection surrounding you.

Breathing into the center of your chest, allow yourself to be touched by the suffering you are experiencing. Feel the heat, darkness, heaviness, sharpness, sad-ness, stuckness, despair, fear, or whatever else is present in your direct experience. Don't be afraid. It won't break your heart; it will open your heart. Breathing out, feel the coolness, brightness, and lightness. Sense any freshness and relief as you repeat these statements to yourself silently, feeling the good intention behind them:

Welcome, dear one. I see your pain. You don't need to be afraid. I will take care of you.

I'm here. I care about your suffering. I will stay with you. I will breathe with you.

It is my wish to care for you wholeheartedly right now, for as long as it takes.

May you be soothed. May you be healed.

I'm sorry you have been ignored and kept away. I will stay with you now and care for you.

I may not always know how to show you that I care, but I am here for you.

When you feel deep sorrow, hopelessness, and despair, I will stay with you. I will breathe with you.

When it is necessary for you to hide, I will wait patiently by your door.

May you be soothed. May you be healed.

When you scream and are on fire with rage, I will stay with you until the fire subsides.

When you appear hardened and impenetrable, I will stand beside you.

May you be soothed. May you be healed.

When you share your most humiliating or murderous accounts, I will not turn away. I will stay with you. I will breathe with you.

May you be soothed. May you be healed.

Once You Have Light

My mind becoming Buddha
Common thoughts have vanished into space;
"Heroic fearlessness" has dawned upon me.
My mind is now identical with Vajradhara.

—YESHE TSOGYAL, *LADY OF THE LOTUS-BORN*

As I commit to healing and political action—as inseparable movements—
I continue to honor my inner life and seek ways to embody liberation.
This involves speaking and protesting; it also emerges in my interper-
sonal relationships with women.

Audre Lorde's fearlessness in transgressing dominant cultural
norms was a force I inhaled at an early age. Like Lorde, I hungered for
mother love. And as with Lorde, my hunger for mother love showed
up in my erotic love for a woman.

She was unlike me in many ways: earthbound, focused on the
tangible world. I was so often cerebral as I basked in the world of
ideas. But she presented as grounded, both supremely confident and
extremely awkward, depending upon the environment in which she
found herself.

She did not read books. In this way more than any other, I was puzzled by my attraction to her. Books were my lifeblood. And yet, I could feel how the sensual energy that flamed around her sparked my experience of my body in a new way. She brought a different way of being—more embodied, not as conceptual—into my vision for the first time in my life as she heightened my sense of maternal love. I craved the affection she offered organically: sweet words, lingering touch. Very quickly, I became more aware of my own stagnant state of mind, my emotional detachment, my overwhelm by enormous expressions of rage. I would retreat into analysis. But she was present, able to show up for the ocean waves that threatened to submerge me. She was able to offer a soothing embrace. She pointed the way to healing deep, familiar wounds.

Years after the friendship ended, I would reflect on our dynamic and other relationships that had offered me aspects of myself that I yearned to embrace. I understood that these women had taken me further. The parts of me that were stuck, mired in fear and intellectual processing, came to the surface and took deep breaths. These women embraced other women with their bodies, boldly and without fear. They took risks. They appeared stable and safe. They exuded mother love.

The Erotic as Power

In the parsing of my relationships with these women, I encountered yet another dimension of Audre Lorde. I had loved her poetry for nearly three decades when I reread *Zami: A New Spelling of My Name*. Lorde referred to this work as a "biomythography"—part memoir, part imagination. I absorbed it over and over again, struck by the vivid descriptions of women's communities and Lorde's own attunement to her desires. She expressed complicated dynamics, including with her own mother, in evocative terms. It was only later, in remembering yet again my relationship with my woman friend, that I thought about how mother love can coexist with sensual connection. I started to appreciate the nuances of Lorde's reflections on erotic power. It was energy that became heightened in the presence of other nurturing women.

I saw in Lorde's embrace of women an echo of James Baldwin's reflections on sensual affection. These two luminaries pointed to same-gender sensual relationships as a way of honoring their inner lives—their feelings, impulses, and capacity for connection. They further uplifted same-gender sexual relationships as a critique of the repressive sexual culture of the United States. While most of this chapter looks at ways in which Audre Lorde uplifted eroticism and female deities as forces for transgressive power, I acknowledge the degree to which Baldwin, too, embraced sensuality as life-giving vitality.

Baldwin's exploration of sexuality is highlighted in the depth of connection he describes in his second novel, *Giovanni's Room*. The two main characters, David and Giovanni, spark an "instantaneous" connection in a Parisian bar. This groundbreaking novel, published in 1955, illuminated an emotional, deeply transformative intimacy that was ultimately fraught because of the broader homophobic Western culture that was their context. Baldwin's main characters attune to each other and mirror one another. In a brief interlude amid social repression, they find each other and are able to resist oppressive, dominant narratives that deem same-gender sexual relationships dirty and shameful.[1]

Life-giving sensuality, touched upon in *Giovanni's Room*, is a thread in other writings by Baldwin. He explores the meaning of blues music for Black Americans by describing the depth of "ironic tenacity" and the suggestion of sensual power. He is most direct in his most well-known book of essays *The Fire Next Time:*

White Americans . . . suspect that the force is sensual, and they are terrified of sensuality and do not any longer understand it.

The word "sensual" is not intended to bring to mind quivering dusky maidens or priapic black studs. I am referring to something much simpler and much less fanciful. To be sensual, I think, is to respect and rejoice in the force of life, of life itself, and to be *present* in all that one does, from the effort of loving to the breaking of bread.[2]

"To be present in all that one does . . ."; I inhaled Baldwin's words. He, like Audre Lorde, was not only offering a critique of the repression inherent in the dominant culture; he was offering a way forward, a suggestion of how to *be* in this complicated, repressive environment in which gender and sexuality are policed by laws and institutions. I heard in Baldwin's reflections a commitment to be in his body, present and responsive, attuned to the world around him. By this time, I was deeply engaged with my Buddhist practice, with rituals that helped me to be in my body (rather than my head), present with how my breath moved like the waves of the ocean. I was practicing taking care of my body. I found that my cerebral tendencies started to balance out when I intentionally took time to honor the way in which my body showed up in the world.

This did not come easily. I first learned forms of Buddhism that had complicated messages about the body and sensuality. Early Buddhism shunned sensual feeling as lustful, a defilement. A later form of Buddhism, Mahayana Buddhism, included many depictions of female deities and bodhisattvas—enlightened beings who forsook full liberation in order to save suffering beings. I appreciated the many expressions of maternal figures in Mahayana Buddhism, but I still experienced the lineages I encountered as repressive, even militaristic. It was in Tibetan Tantric Buddhism that I found echoes of Baldwin and Lorde's embrace of sensual energy and power. Tibetan Tantric Buddhism honors sensuality—with training—as a source of wisdom. The tradition contains female images known as *dakini*. I observed correlations between the dakini in Tantric Buddhism and the West African mother-goddesses embraced by Audre Lorde.

Tantric Buddhism and Audre Lorde

Lorde claimed female and nonbinary African deities as a core part of her spiritual practice. Although I see many aspects of her practice as similar to Tibetan Tantric Buddhism, I do not suggest that Audre Lorde's writings directly convey the intricacies and nuances of the Buddhist tradition. The history of Tantric Buddhism is long and complex and varies according to specific deities, locations, and lineages. It is important to examine it on its own terms. Similarly, it is critical to consider Lorde's work on her own terms, in her own context. I am not attempting to collapse her ideas into Tibetan Tantric Buddhism, or to conflate the esoteric intricacies of Tibetan Tantric Buddhism with Lorde's writings. But I seek to illuminate the connections.

I acknowledge that the process of bringing together Lorde's embrace of West African female deities with Tibetan Tantric Buddhist traditions is messy. I am attempting to put traditions, spiritual practices, and divine beings from different centuries and environments into conversation. These traditions are highly specific, but in my own experience, encountering them has helped illuminate the ways in which female, erotic energy fuels transgressive, powerful ways of being in patriarchal spheres.

I am conscious that my attempts to bring together Tibetan Tantric Buddhism with Lorde's spirituality can be seen as "orientalist"— gazing at a tradition that I have only peripherally practiced from a distant, Western lens. Lorde, herself, was critiqued by African scholars for appropriating African religious traditions that were not hers, and evolving them in ways that were incongruent with their cultural origins, meanings, and contexts.

I also acknowledge that sexual abuse within many lineages of Buddhism is increasingly being made known. In honoring sensuality—in Lorde's writings as well as in Tantric texts—I do not ignore the harm enacted in transgressing sexual boundaries and exploiting students in uneven power dynamics. It is not my intention to minimize or ignore abuse. For that reason, perhaps, I pay less attention to the relationship between the teacher/guru and the practitioner, even as this relationship is at the center of the practice of enlightenment within Zen lineages as well as Tibetan Tantric Buddhism. The boundaries between guru and student are crucial to maintain.

But I uplift Tibetan Tantric Buddhism because while researching deity yoga in the Tibetan Tantric tradition, I heard Lorde in a new way. Although I had read her work for decades, and even annotated her book of poems *The Black Unicorn*, I had glossed over Lorde's references to West African deities. Later, after starting a Buddhist practice, I observed that much of what Lorde pointed to—such as the maternal, warrior spirit embedded in West African religions and her practice of visualizing herself as a deity—have corresponding ritual practices within Tibetan Tantric Buddhism.

Because Tantric Buddhism is an esoteric practice, many aspects of it remain unknown and impenetrable. References in Tantric texts are not easily translatable or understood. Yet encountering the teachings of Tibetan Tantric Buddhism, even on a superficial level, sparked in me a deepening understanding of Lorde's work. Lorde's writings emphasize power and transgression, specifically, *the power of transgression*, in a way that helps me understand the liberatory thrust of Tibetan Tantric teachings within the ever-evolving Buddhist canon.

I identified the power of Audre Lorde's life—her words and activism—as that which arose from her practice of honoring West African female deities. She exhibited defiance in her early years as she resisted the patriarchy and expectations of obedience in her household. Before she traveled to West Africa in 1974, she chose to be in same-gender loving relationships. She contested racism in the second-generation feminist movement and sexism in the Black freedom movement. All of this resistance to hegemonic norms became more spiritually grounded and coherent when she encountered Fon, Dahomey, and Yoruba religious traditions.

As she embraced female West African deities, she imagined herself as one. In my eyes, Lorde's adoption of African deities, especially one whom she called "Afrekete," was very obviously subversive: By embracing dark-skinned, female-bodied images, she implicitly rejected white, male, Christian norms.

In this way, Lorde showed me the power of transgression. She uplifted Black mother-warriors as powerful. She reversed the image of that which was deemed defiled and fear-inducing. My appearance had been deemed polluted in my mother's white family, but in Lorde's world, my dark, female body was celebrated.

"The Erotic Offers a Well of Replenishing and Provocative Force"

Audre Lorde's embrace of erotic power shone a light on a concept central to Tibetan Tantric Buddhism: Sensuality, practiced with Right View, can be embraced as a path to liberation. This idea is articulated in a range of Lorde's works, starting with her "biomythography" *Zami: A New Spelling of My Name*. It is also at the heart of her essay "Uses of the Erotic: The Erotic as Power" as well as numerous poems on women's relationships. During her adult life, Lorde partook in creating lesbian communities in New York City. While these collectives were marginalized and disproportionately policed by dominant heteronormative institutions, they and the other lesbian communities that emerged in the 1950s sought to create safe, culturally expansive spaces.

These spaces, and the gatherings that took place in them, fostered sensual power, one that privileges new ways of seeing the female body as that which is inherently authoritative on its own terms. It is not merely an object to serve the purposes and aspirations of those who perpetuate the dominant culture.[3] Rather, the female body is honored in its own right: It is a dark, complex, mysterious manifestation of erotic energy in the world. Lorde wrote:

> The erotic offers a well of replenishing and provocative force to the woman who does not fear its revelation, nor succumb to the belief that sensation is enough. . . . For the erotic is not a question only of what we do; it is a question of how acutely and fully we can feel in the doing. Once we know the extent to which we are capable of feeling that sense of satisfaction and completion, we can then observe which of our various life endeavors bring us closest to that fullness.[4]

Lorde embraced the transgressive—and therefore dangerous—nature of the erotic. She continued: "When I speak of the erotic, then, I speak of it as an assertion of the lifeforce of women; of that creative energy empowered, the knowledge and use of which we are now reclaiming in our language, our history, our dancing, our loving, our work, our lives."[5]

For Lorde, eroticism as a life force is explicitly spiritual, which she described as "psycho-emotional." She was careful to refuse dualisms; she did not contrast the white male body with the Black female body. Nor did she polarize the rationality associated with European-derived patriarchy with the emotions correlated with the Black mother. Rather, she included the white male body in her expansive worldview, stating: "I'm not saying . . . that white does not feel. I'm saying that we must amalgamate the two, never close our eyes to the terror, the chaos which is black which is creative which is female which is dark which is rejected which is messy which is . . . sinister, smelly, erotic, confused, upsetting."[6]

The revaluing of Black women's bodies, and the sensuality that pervades them, is a counterweight to the patriarchal mythology that harms women. In claiming women's bodies as sensual, Lorde was able to see her own energies in an entirely new way. In a 1979 interview, Lorde affirmed:

> Love is . . . a source of tremendous power. Women have not been taught to respect the erotic urge, the place that is uniquely female . . . we, as women, tend to reject our capacity for feeling,

our ability to love, to touch the erotic, because it has been deval-
ued. But it is within this that lies so much of our power, our
ability to posit, to vision. Because once we know how deeply
we can feel, we begin to demand from all of our life pursuits
that they be in accordance with these feelings. . . . When you
live always in darkness, when you live without the sunlight, you
don't know what it is to relish the bright light or even to have
too much of it. Once you have light, then you can measure its
degree. So too with joy.[7]

Eroticism—and the depth of feeling underlying it—served Lorde's
evolving self-definition. So too did the pantheon of African deities she
internalized.

"Becoming. Afrekete."

In her book of poems *The Black Unicorn*, Lorde drew upon the maternal, sensual female and gender-fluid deities that she encountered
during her 1974 trip to West Africa. She often referred to each one
individually as "mother-goddess of all." She was especially drawn to
Yemanjá, the Yoruba goddess of the sea, and Seboulisa, a mother-
goddess of Abomey who is considered a local representation of
Mawulisa.[8] Lorde saw herself in them. In one poem, "The Winds of
Orisha," Lorde merged her voice with Seboulisa, who, for Lorde, embodied an archetypal African foremother.[9] Seboulisa aids speech and con-
trasts silence with life-altering words. In her poem "125th Street and
Abomey," Lorde described Seboulisa as a "mother-goddess with one
breast/eaten away by worms of sorrow and loss."[10]

In the second stanza of "The Winds of Orisha," Lorde inscribed:
"I become myself an incantation."[11] The poem evokes core themes for
Lorde: touch and sensual embodiment; maternal embrace and birth,
and of course, the power of the mother-goddess. Above all, "Winds of
Orisha" speaks of disruption. Legends change the earth's formation.
"Dark and raucous characters" leap across "bland pages." Shango roars

out of the seas. The earth shakes. The winds warn. Oya destroys tidiness. Eshu's "Black laughter / turns up the neat sleeping sand." In a 1986 conversation, Lorde elaborated:

> Yemanjá is the mother of us all. She is the aura of goddess, of rivers, of love, and of war. And ["From the House of Yemanjá"] really deals not only with the split consciousness that so many light skinned Black women from the islands have, but also how it is necessary for each one of us to claim all of the parts of our ancestry, and at the same time to recognize the great nourishment and the great power of our Blackness. The Black mother being the source of nourishment, the source of power for us all—black, white, male, and female.[12]

Lorde also identified with the goddess Mawulisa (also spelled MawuLisa and Mawu-Lisa), whom she referred to as "thunder, sky, sun, the great mother of us all." Mawulisa is mother to the god Eshu, also known as "Elegba" and "Elegbara," the youngest and most clever of her sons.[13] Although male-bodied, in dance performances, his part is danced by a woman with an attached phallus.[14] Eshu is exhibited as gender fluid and is not restricted to human distinctions of gender; Eshu is at once both male and female.[15] This gender fluidity was important for Lorde. One of Lorde's biographers, Alexis De Veaux observes, "As [Lorde] traveled through West Africa, her search for an ancestral female self, for 'some woman legends,' became the basis for a deeper realization of the unity of the male and female energies in African thought, if not practice. That unity was the erotic core of an African ancestral self."[16] Lorde spoke to her desire for male-female union directly in the Prologue of her biomythography *Zami*: "I have always wanted to be both man and woman, to incorporate the strongest and richest parts of my mother and father within/into me—to share valleys and mountains upon my body the way the earth does in hills and peaks."[17]

The gender-fluid Eshu was, therefore, for Lorde a spiritual ancestor. Furthermore, he is a skillful trickster who uses language unpredictably and subverts traditional authority figures and institutions. Such subversion was compelling for Lorde in her struggle against oppressive belief systems and behaviors in her parents' home, in Catholic school, in the workplace, and in broader patriarchal society.[18] She found in the trickster image a model for linguistic confrontation and subversion. Kara Provost reflects: "Building upon the trickster's tradition of sensuality, ambiguity, and transgression of boundaries, rules, and inhibitions allows Lorde to reclaim the repressed power and pleasure of female eroticism—even (or especially) as a woman who loves women."[19]

Like Eshu, Lorde claimed a way of being that was simultaneously subversive and erotic. And like Yemanjá and Mawulisa, the great mothers, she claimed a way of being that was at once maternal and sensual. But, as aforementioned, the African goddess with whom she most resonated was the Ewe-Fon sea-goddess Avrekete, whom Lorde referred to as "Afrekete" in poetry, correspondence, and her biomythography *Zami*. Afrekete knows all the languages of the gods.[20] Afrekete is the youngest child, destined to be the most intelligent, according to Yoruba and Fon traditions.[21] This youngest daughter description of Afrekete aligned with Lorde's own experience as the youngest—and most rebellious—of her parents' three daughters.

As a female-bodied figure, Afrekete refutes the dominant culture's definitions merely by existing in the world. She is at once an African goddess and a language maker, a Black woman warrior and a poet, a sensual trickster and a mother.[22] She is dangerous, Lorde acknowledged.[23] She represents protectiveness and rupture.

As Lorde looked to Afrekete as a guide for subverting hegemonic norms, she sought to merge with Afrekete metaphorically and psychologically. In this way, Lorde conceptualized of her own self as a Black goddess. In the dedication of *Zami: A New Spelling of My Name*, Lorde declared: "To the hands of Afrekete." She stated a few pages later:

To the journeywoman pieces of myself.
Becoming.
Afrekete.[24]

Later, in the conclusion of *Zami,* Lorde wrote: "Afrekete, [Mawuli-sa's] youngest daughter, the mischievous linguist, trickster, best-beloved, whom we must all become."[25]

Ahn Hua summarizes Lorde's practice of visualizing herself as a sensual, subversive African goddess—as Afrekete—as authoritative self-transformation.

> Embodied in the figure of Afrekete is the combination of an Afri-can goddess, the sexy black woman with whom Lorde has an affair, Lorde herself as an oppositional writer, and the coming together of writing and lesbian eroticism through individual and collective erotic embodied remembrance. By beginning and ending the memoir with the image of Afrekete, Lorde has "incor-porated the subversive (and sexy) trickster into her own identity in the process of writing her autobiography; she has rebirthed herself not only as the collective *Zami* but also as the mischie-vous, linguist/writer Afrekete, who will reach deep into the often repressed powers of female sexuality to fuel her writing."[26]

By internalizing Afrekete and other African goddesses, Lorde expanded a depth of spirituality within her own psyche that led her to "recognize the sacredness of her own female power."[27] The youngest, darkest, most rebellious daughter could harness her oppositional energy and envision herself as divine. This was itself a revolutionary act.

Indeed, imagining oneself as a female deity was a generative, even explosive, challenge to the dominant culture of 1970s and 1980s Amer-ica. By embracing African goddesses—and internalizing a sense of her own dark, female power—Lorde refuted institutional norms. This included ideas within the predominantly white feminist movement, such as those promulgated by white theologian Mary Daly.[28] Further-more, no longer were Black women solely valued for reproduction.[29] Nor did they exist to be used for white America's gain. Lorde's embrace of female African deities was at once resistance to the status quo and the act of standing on her own terms. She saw herself anew, beyond the despised Black child and the exploited Black woman. She refused to adapt to prevailing cultural constructions; instead she claimed a "Black lesbian feminist poet warrior mother" identity that arose from divinely inspired imagery.[30] She employed imagination, dreams, and visualization as she identified a sacredness in her dark skin, her lesbian identity, her erotic way of being.

I could feel the intensity of Lorde's imagination as I read once again Lorde's poems and biomythography. I understood more deeply how erotic energy underlies every aspect of mother-warriorship and trickster weaponry.

As I meditated on the deities to whom Lorde had introduced me—especially Yemanjá—I found that in my own practice, the deities assumed forms related to the natural world: rivers, mountains, seas. I imagined a green female goddess with hair like a river; a narrow brown goddess who moved as if she were a seed bursting from a pod. These goddesses appeared as shimmery, marinated in light. They retained the maternal soft energy that was so compelling to me.

Could I imagine myself *becoming* a mother-goddess, as Lorde had done? This was more difficult for me. I found myself in a state of exertion rather than soft visualization when I attempted these practices. But I could also feel a shift taking place over time, an energy that was previously unnamable or perhaps inaccessible despite two decades of meditation. I found myself more willing to draw boundaries with people who sought to use and exploit me. I had been raised as a caretaker and had developed default settings for taking care of other adults, often at my own expense. This often involved self-silencing in order to make other people feel comfortable, not threatened or angry. While envisioning Yemanjá, and even considering that I might *become* her, I began to see my self-silencing, enabling patterns more clearly. I began to see myself as a mother-warrior. Not a goddess. But deeply, fiercely protective, of myself and other vulnerable people. I started to say out loud: *I refuse to be exploited. I am protective, a mother-warrior.*

This was a shift in my own sense of power. Visualizing mother-goddesses created a source of enormous capacity for me.

"They Were Loving, But They Were Also Really Tough Warriors"

The power that Lorde attained in claiming African deities as her own—as she saw herself in them and of them—fostered a deep sense of ancestral lineages. De Veaux notes that "Lorde was convinced that a maternal, spiritual bloodline had been revealed to her in Dahomey— one which had been subconscious, but which was now a useful conscious reality."[31] Furthermore, embracing West African goddesses as part of her ancestral lineage connected Lorde to her biological mother and the Black women of her childhood.

In a 1986 interview, Lorde reflected:

> I called [*Zami*] a biomythography because it is not only autobiography. It also partakes of myths and history and a lot of other ways we use knowledge; and I use those myths in *Zami* . . . it is the West African women of Dahomey who have the legend . . . Dahomeyan amazons who were the fiercest warriors of the king. It is very important to have that, because, in fact, in the lives of so many Afro-American women, my mother, my mother's generation, I saw these women were nurturing, they were cherishing, they were loving, but they were also really tough warriors, you know. So, we need to know that that is part of our tradition.[32]

One of Lorde's biographers, Alexis Pauline Gumbs, refers to this process as "a poetics of black queer maternity, a reimagining of 'connection, accountability, and the production of a livable world.'"[33] This poetic way of being, which is, at once, dangerous, transgressive, and generative, is also authoritative. The sensual Black mother-goddess is a spiritual force that cannot be ignored, evaded, or repressed: She is a protective force with which the dominant culture must contend. She remains subversive by her very embodiment as she denounces the violence of a patriarchal world.

"Achieving the Fulfillment of Our Tremendous Potential"

I saw within Lorde's spiritual journey a mirroring of Tibetan Tantric practices of deity yoga. Tibetan Tantric Buddhism teaches that human beings experience delusion and confusion, but that the essential nature of the human being is clear and pure.[34] The practice of deity yoga aids in cutting through the temporary afflictions of anxiety and confusion. Practitioners—with the guidance of a guru—meditate on the figure of a deity and seek to manifest the deity. Tibetan Buddhologist Jan Willis, quoting her teacher Lama Thubten Yeshe, explains that "deity yoga is one of the most profound ways of lifting our self-image, and . . . achieving the fulfillment of our tremendous potential."[35]

Lama Yeshe implicitly draws a link between Tibetan Tantrism and Audre Lorde's orientation toward "becoming Afrekete." In his text *Introduction to Tantra: The Transformation of Desire,* he acknowledges that "emanating yourself as a deity has nothing to do with a particular culture or a particular set of beliefs."[36]

Lama Yeshe's reflections are shared by Buddhist Studies scholars.[37] Visualization is a practice in which a deity is conjured from a still mind. The qualities of the deity are internalized by chanting mantras and other prayers associated with that deity.

Lama Yeshe instructs:

When you see yourself as a deity, you should feel that you are the real emanation of the deity. Don't think that you are just pretending; you should be convinced. Then, like the actor who remains in character even after the play is finished, you might surprise yourself to find that you have actually become the deity. Such divine pride—the strong sense of actually being the deity—is crucial. With it, tantric transformation will come naturally and be very powerful. Those people who think that tantra is only involved with pretending to be a deity are completely mistaken.[38]

I saw this practice in Audre Lorde's depiction of herself as Afrekete. She sought to envision herself as the "real emanation of the deity." I imagined her as a mother-warrior, a female being with a baby strapped to her back and a weapon in her hand. I appreciated that range of protectiveness: the softness and fierceness, enmeshed.

"Silence Is a Contract Made Between Oppressor and Oppression"

Lorde was deeply attuned to the terror embedded in state violence against Black bodies. As she internalized Black female deities and saw herself as one, she also asserted transgressive ways of challenging society. Lorde embraced her role as a linguistic trickster, a poet who uses words skillfully to confront myopia and official terror—in our society as well as in ourselves. This is seen starkly in her poem "Power." "The difference between poetry and rhetoric / is being ready to kill / yourself / instead of your children," she wrote. Poetry requires risk. It propels us to feel the full extent of rage, in which the blood of a Black child who has been killed by a white police officer is the only liquid in the "whiteness / of the desert where I am lost / without imagery or magic." It forces us to reckon with our fear and our self-silencing, the coercions that propel us to give up our power.[39]

Lorde confronted the violence of white delusion, as well as the sole Black woman who went along with the complacency of the eleven white jurors who refuse to hold the white police officer accountable for murder. She used multiple voices and wordplay to disrupt the status quo.[40] She sought to "write fire until it comes out of my ears, my eyes, my nose holes—everywhere. Until it's every breath I breathe."[41]

In a 1987 interview, Lorde described a story of a Black girl swept across the street with fire hoses. The scene was horrific. It had to be called out as such. Lorde elaborated: "That's why poetry is the most subversive use of language there is, because it's about changing feelings."[42] Poetry transgresses the norms established by institutional violence—norms that seek to hide truths and numb people—by thrusting into view the rage that follows gross injustices. Poetry refuses to let a deluge of information and institutional pressure overwhelm people. It provokes feeling as a natural response to the massive harms that are taking place; it provides a way to channel one's power. Lorde continued:

> I know that I always felt very committed to using my power . . . but it was not until I began to break my own silences, to recognize that those silences existed, that they were not serving me, that [I realized that] silence did not protect me . . . to translate that silence first into language and then into action had to be the point of empowering myself. So I would say it is absolutely necessary to break silence, to give a certain form to those things that we wish, first of all, to change and even more importantly to give form to those things which we wish to create. . . . We must be able to take out of our desires and our visions a template for a pattern for the future.[43]

Such internalized power fuels women's capacity to dream and willingness to speak as protective, determined warriors.

Confronting Patriarchy: The Dakini in Tibetan Tantric Buddhism

In her fierce confrontations of violence and her embodiment of transgressive power, Lorde mirrors yet another aspect of Tibetan Tantric Buddhism: the figure of the *dakini*. A feminine image of transgressive wisdom, the dakini is depicted as a naked, female-bodied being who wears a necklace of skulls and carries a skullcap filled with blood. She is simultaneously a sensual and maternal figure who conveys clarity and compassion.

In Tibetan Buddhism, the dakini functions as a messenger of freedom and an embodiment of wisdom. She offers energies that practitioners can invoke to transform a meditation practice. Dakinis are protectors on the spiritual path, teachers who awaken. Jan Willis writes, "within Buddhist tantric contexts, *dakini* is viewed as the supreme embodiment of the highest wisdom itself."[44]

In sacred biographies, the dakini is depicted as an unpredictable, semi-wrathful, dancing spirit-woman who appears in visions, dreams, or the everyday lives of practitioners. Her demeanor changes in various contexts: She may be playful and nurturing, or sharp and wrathful. The dakini represents the domains conventionally attributed to women, such as embodiment, sexuality, nurture and sustenance, and relationship. Yet, these domains are transmuted into realms that are much more profound than the concerns of daily existence.

For Tantric practitioners, the dakini is the inner catalyst, protagonist, and witness of the spiritual journey. Judith Simmer-Brown describes the *dakini* as "the most potent realized essence of every being, the inner awakening, and the gift of the Buddha."[45] This is a provocative image. In confronting isolation and transforming desolation into wisdom, the dakinis reflect an enlightened, sacred female divinity that is naked, truthful, fierce, active, dancing, wild, and free.

I saw Audre Lorde as a dakini. Moreover, I saw within Lorde's embrace of Yemanjá, Seboulisa, and Afrekete parallel images of sensual, maternal wisdom. As I dove more deeply into Lorde's poetry and her biomythography *Zami*, I sought to embody this energy in my own life. I cultivated a daily practice that mirrored the visualization practices of Lorde and Tibetan Tantric Buddhists. I did not call my practice a "dakini practice" or "deity yoga," or explicitly identify my cultivation of transgressive, maternal energy with a particular Buddhist tradition.

I referred to my meditation as "taking refuge" as I had been trained in the Insight tradition, but with a deeper orientation toward sensual, wild, maternal energy and ancestral connection.

This was a way of cultivating protection and safety, of creating a foundation from which disruption could emerge. In my meditation practice, I brought forth Audre Lorde's words: *We can learn to mother ourselves.* This mother energy, mother love, was the mother-warrior-goddess energy of West African deities, as well as dakini spirituality enlivened in the Tibetan Tantric tradition. Protective. Guiding. Fierce. It made sense to me, too, that it was heightened in erotic, maternal encounters. The transgressive, maternal goddess-dakini energy that arose in my practice offered stability and consistency, a refuge. This energy could encircle the grief that underlay so much of my life, beginning with my grandparents' rejection of my existence, my mother's lack of protection and attention, my father's abandonment of me, and my complete disconnection from his lineage. The mother-goddess Yemanjá, the Great Mother dakini that arose in my practice, manifested as softness that was, at the same time, both transgressive and powerful.

This mother dakini legitimized anger at the same time she legitimized grief. She was outraged at injustice. Perhaps most importantly, she offered consistent compassion. Audre Lorde's embrace of the West African goddesses Seboulisa and Afrekete made sense to me. They were mothers. They were warriors. And Afrekete, too, represented a kind of sensual energy that Lorde connected to sexuality and same-gender loving relationships. The erotic, for Lorde, was fundamentally a life-giving energy.

I celebrated the images of mother beings in both Tibetan Tantric and West African traditions. I recognized the sophistication of West African cultures that had been dismissed as backward and inferior through a Western gaze, yet that retained, over centuries, powerful women-centered ways of enacting power. I saw a contemporary manifestation of these teachings in Audre Lorde's insistence on erotic power at a time when claiming lesbian identity was anathema in the Black freedom movement, and loving Blackness was marginalized in the second-generation feminist movement.

These female-bodied figures—the dakini and the West African goddesses—were powerful images whose depiction of sensuality, righteous wrath, and maternal compassion made them spiritual guides in their own right. They were soft and they were fierce. Above all, they were protective and free. Honoring them fostered transgressive power that provoked me to confront oppressive violence and silencing.

PRACTICE
Sadhana of Awakened Melanin

The following practice of summoning deities was developed by Justin Miles, a teacher in the Shambhala lineage.[46] I practiced this *sadhana* (Buddhist prayer) with Justin and seventy-five other Black Buddhists in November 2019 during a "Fierce Urgency of Now" retreat in Northern California. It was profound to collectively call upon African warrior spirits within a Buddhist prayer. While these are not the traditional deity practices that I allude to in this chapter, they are adaptations of *sadhanas* in the Shambhala lineage that invoke African deities and figures.

"INVITATION TO THE DIVINE"
MEDITATION BY JUSTIN MILES

Close your eyes and invite the divine (whatever you consider to be divine—your God [or Goddess], higher power, deity, ancestors, etc.) to be present with you right now. Feel their presence around and within you: front, back, sides, underneath, above, and within. Engage in this feeling of contemplation, returning again and again to this experience of sacredness.

(Gong)

(Recite)

Let all divine and sacred beings be present

Inside

Between

And as all things

The alpha and the omega are never in different times

Only now

If my divine is real, then my divine is now

If my divine is now and my mind is elsewhere, then my divine is not realized, it is assumed

The mind of greed, passion, fear, anger, pride, jealousy, doubt, and ignorance is elsewhere

The mind that sees the divine in all beings is relaxed and attentive

The mind that sees the divine between all beings is relaxed and attentive

The mind that sees the divine in all things is relaxed and attentive

All else is talk and ideas

Which have never built families, schools, communities, cultures, or friendships

The basis for these things is awareness of ever-present goodness

Therefore, let all divine beings be present but let us be present with all divine beings.

(Gong)

Rest in the presence of the collective energy of all divine present in the space. Do not talk or listen for messages. Rest in the feeling. Do not describe it. Just feel within, between, and as all things. Arise with an integrated sense of divine presence however that resonates with or manifests for you.

LIBATION IN CELEBRATION OF
THE UNIVERSAL LINEAGE OF WARRIORSHIP

Commentary

All of us come from families or have been influenced by those who could be called warriors; not warrior in the sense of violence or war (even though your ancestor may have manifested bravery in combat), but warrior in the sense of cultivating and manifesting a good heart and being of benefit to others—the real, tough work. This practice asks us to invite those warriors into the space and asks them to bless us with their wisdom and warmth. When we do that as a community, it is a time for celebration—a family reunion of sorts. We are celebrating each other's ancestors and the joy of sharing and learning. We listen to who is important to others and make room in our minds and hearts for others' ancestors.

The pouring of libations is a ritual that is Afrikan in origin and involves remembering our ancestors and asking their essence, minds, and hearts to be present with us. It is similar to the ancient Tibetan ceremony called a *lhasang* in that it invokes the energy of an ancestral force whose energy we recognize as being no different than our own fundamental nature. We use water as a symbol of inherent purity and clarity. When the elder pours the water into the vessel or the earth, it symbolizes joining our pure nature with that of our ancestors.

This practice brings together two warrior lineages: the Ifá tradition of West Africa and the Shambhala Warrior lineage. Both paths utilize the principle of Ashe and share a similar meaning: affirming an understanding of things as they are at their nature. When we say "Ashe!" we cut through our conceptual mind and affirm the presence of our ancestors, experience confidence, and feel energized.

(Recite monotone and monosyllabic)

(Gong/deaden)

When the confidence which is primordially free

Was followed and delighted in

Countless multitudes of warriors arose.

(O>o)

(Gong)

(Begin drumming slowly for first three syllables then steadily)

    In remembrance and celebration

    of the human manifestations of basic goodness

    both here on this land and throughout the world

    we pour libation to those ancestors who through their

    fearlessness and gentleness

    helped to liberate all sentient beings from ignorance and suffering

    so that enlightened society could manifest in the ten directions

    Through the power of your blessings may we manifest wisdom, compassion,

    and discipline so that we may follow your example in all spheres of life

    awakening all whom we encounter through skillful means

    a noble heart of compassion and authentic presence

    father and mother lineages, recognize us your children

    as the dawn (Gong) of the Great Afrikan Sun

    invoking your energy, we take the form of those who have gone before

    and raise the banner of Enlightened Society

    in the name of the unbroken Universal Lineage of Warriorship

(O>o)

(Gong)

(Recite)

    We pour in remembrance to those ancestors, foremothers, and forefathers

    in all our homelands, originators of the races and cultures of basic
    goodness

    and we all say: Ashe!

(Gong)

    We pour in remembrance to those ancestors destroyed in atrocities, wars,

    enslavement, oppression, and so on

may their bloodshed never be forgotten

and we all say: Ashe!

(Gong)

We pour in remembrance to those ancestors of this land on which we
reside

the native, enslaved, and migrant caretakers and warriors of this place

and we all say: Ashe!

(Gong)

We pour in remembrance of those ancestors

our heroes and sheroes whose influence in our lives

planted the seeds of courage, compassion, and wisdom

the bodhisattva warrior's path of aspiring and entering

O noble ones we call out your names

to honor your accomplishments

that we may continue your legacy

of sanity and vision for all sentient beings.

Call out the name of your ancestors or anyone who had a profound impact on
your life who is no longer living, to invoke their energy of compassion, courage,
and wisdom. After any name is said, all should say "Ashe!" The gong should be
rung steadily throughout this part, and water should be poured for each name, for
about two minutes, or until the calling of names is complete. It should be left to the
senior teacher or student present as to when the calling of names should cease.
After all names have been called, rest in the presence of your ancestors, contemplating their influence in your life.

(Begin slowly on "In" and draw out the word. Ex. Innnnn . . .)

In complete remembrance of the warriors throughout time and space

of our own lineage and others who embody the principles of awakened

heart, fearlessness, the transcendent actions and so forth, named, and

unnamed,

born, and yet to be born, we pour three times to the unbroken Universal Lineage of Warriorship in the past present and future

Ashe! Ashe! Ashe!

(Each "Ashe!" is said slowly)

(Gong after each "Ashe!")

Personal Power That Moves Us

When I speak of power, I am speaking of personal power on a continuum. That is to say, not merely personal power that concentrates itself in, but personal power which moves us.

—AUDRE LORDE

Not everything that is faced can be changed, but nothing can be changed until it is faced.

—JAMES BALDWIN

I began this book gripped with questions on how to respond to genocide taking place in Gaza. As I wrestled with my fear of speaking out and as I summoned the courage to take action, I drew upon the wisdom of Audre Lorde, James Baldwin, and the Buddha. Time and again, I went to the cushion for refuge and went to my desk to write.

I wrote through all of 2024. At the end of 2024, the forty-seventh president was elected. He had already proclaimed on the campaign trail that on day one, he would be a "dictator." And so it is. As I complete this manuscript, one hundred days after his inauguration, groups to which I belong and governmental systems for which I pay taxes are under attack.

The forty-seventh president has initiated raids on undocumented and documented immigrants and disappeared hundreds of individuals and families to other countries, including a supermax prison in El Salvador. He has directed plainclothes, masked immigration officers to arrest and detain scholars who advocate for Palestinian rights. He has withdrawn billions of dollars in research grants from universities and sought to control university autonomy. He has signed an executive order to defund and dismantle Diversity, Equity, and Inclusion programs in all government-funded agencies and institutions. He has signed an executive order refusing to recognize the existence of transgender persons and to deny them gender-specific medical treatment. This is deeply personal for me.

The forty-seventh president has cut off grants for medical research, defunded the Centers for Disease Control, and shut down USAID, threatening millions of lives that depend on life-giving humanitarian assistance around the world. He is attempting to dismantle the Department of Education, which, among other important services, offers would-be college and graduate students student loan support. He is attempting to decimate the civil service workforce. With the technical support of the richest man in the world, who bankrolled 47's campaign to the tune of $290 million, he has made vulnerable sensitive information in the office of the US Treasury.

And the assault is just beginning. He has announced his desire to "own" and ethnically cleanse the Gaza Strip, to displace 2.3 million Palestinians in the process, so that he can develop the Gaza Strip as a beachfront "Riviera."

How do we confront this onslaught, beyond expressing fear and outrage? We can get stuck in cycles of reactivity, always caught off guard, unable to stand on our own feet and set our own terms. I draw upon the fierce, protective mother-warrior energy of Audre Lorde. I use my anger. This rage is a poison that can nourish us, can be metabolized for growth and change. *We must not be silent. We must speak, remembering, we were never meant to survive.*

Lorde faced the violence and named it. She used trickster language to stand up to it. She did not back down.

And she retained such stamina because she turned toward her own person and her own community and affirmed worth, both individually and collectively. She used her anger as energy for growth. It did not burn like a wildfire; she trained it with accuracy.

And Baldwin, too, confronted white violence with precision. He studied the white mind and saw the pretentious hollowness, the lies. He dismissed the false morality of the white world. He did not react impulsively, but rather, he set his own terms. He was a Black man who moved out of his place. In the very act of seeing through whiteness, Baldwin resisted white violence. He was angry. But he resisted the violence from a place of compassion. He wrote to his nephew in 1962 that Black people should accept white people with love. That was a tall order in 1962, and it is a tall order today. But I hear the wisdom of Baldwin's words. We must know the mind of the oppressive forces but refuse to operate on their terms. We can choose a different path. We *must* choose a different path: not to replicate the hollowness of white morality, but to turn toward our own lives, to know our pain intimately, to use it for fuel, with compassion.

In knowing the white mind ("the white problem"), Baldwin said, we have to take into account just how earth-shattering it is to assert Black excellence:

> [White people] are, in effect, still trapped in a history which they do not understand; and until they understand it, they cannot be released from it. They have had to believe for many years, and for innumerable reasons, that black men are inferior to white men. . . . In this case, the danger, in the minds of most white Americans, is the loss of their identity. Try to imagine how you would feel if you woke up one morning to find the sun shining and all the stars aflame. You would be frightened because it is out of the order of nature. Any upheaval in the universe is terrifying because it so profoundly attacks one's sense

of one's own reality. Well, the black man has functioned in the white man's world as a fixed star, as an immovable pillar: and as he moves out of his place, heaven and earth are shaken to their foundations.[1]

I remember Baldwin's prescient words as I read of a high-level placement at the US state department in the first few weeks of the 47th administration. This official had posted on social media just four months prior: "Competent white men must be in charge if you want things to work. Unfortunately, our entire national ideology is predicated on coddling the feelings of women and minorities, and demoralizing competent white men."[2] But it was this white supremacist's further remarks that reminded me of Baldwin: He said that Black lawmakers, policymakers, and groups need to "learn" their place and take "a knee to MAGA."[3] Among other Black officials and public intellectuals that he attacked, he wrote: "Ibram Kendi needs to learn his place and take a knee to MAGA. Learn his proper role in our society."[4]

Black people have moved to the center of society, out of our "place," and fragile white men cannot take it. This is a familiar worldview to me—I grew up hearing it from my grandparents—but through Baldwin's eyes, I understand it more clearly.

He saw white fragility for what it is. Baldwin, in responding to overt expressions of white superiority, nonetheless did not react in kind. I have tremendous respect for Baldwin's refusal to give back what he had been handed. He was not going to drop to the low rungs of white morality; he was going to operate on his own terms, by his own standards. It required a tremendous amount of emotional labor. But he used everything—the hatred and vitriol, the humiliations and disregard—as kindling for his own inner fire. And he trained his fire with precision, with love.

I draw deep breaths when I read their works alongside news of the white violence emanating from the White House. I am reminded of my mother's parents and their hatred; I am aware of my role as a mother and protector. The work in front of me, using Baldwin's and Lorde's words as a guide, is to *metabolize*—to turn toward it all, rather than shut down. I draw upon Buddhist doctrine and practice: clear seeing, deep compassion, envisioning mother-goddesses, coming back to my body as refuge, again and again.

And it is incumbent upon me to find other people who are doing the same work.

As I conclude the writing of this book, I have gathered with other activists who are focused on stopping the genocide and ethnic cleansing of Palestine and are actively supporting the well-being of Palestinians in Gaza and the West Bank. Our work is deeply personal, and it is also collective. We need each other.

And I have continued to invest in creating a community where I live. After a hurricane destroyed my home city of Asheville, North Carolina, a group of practitioners of the "global majority" found each other.[5] We have started to form a little sangha that is deeply committed to the liberation of Palestine as well as our own liberation. We see our fates as deeply intertwined.

So much of my healing work has been turning toward my family wounds. I draw upon Audre Lorde's protective mother-warrior energy when I examine the hatred that deformed my early years. But it is not the final story. Over the course of writing this book, I hired a private investigator. It was four months after I learned of my father's death, after trying for several days to track down the names of family members using various reports and websites. I hit roadblocks. I needed help.

I took the plunge. I contacted a company that tracked down birth parents of adopted children. I had a DNA test in hand and enough data to find distant relatives. The investigators were immediately excited. I shared almost 4 percent of my DNA with two second cousins. At the time, I did not know this fact was significant. But one investigator, who specializes in DNA research, was optimistic. She promised that she could find out my grandmother's name.

I gave her all of the information that I had. And then I went on an eight-night silent retreat. It was a period in which I sat with tremendous anxiety, day after day. I slept poorly. I could feel my stress increase each morning. All I could do was turn toward my distress and bring compassionate, soothing energy to the thoughts that arose in my mind.

It was in the Newark airport security line, returning home from the retreat, that the fearlessness I sought began to manifest. I received a text from the investigator. She had found my family.

I sat at the gate, receiving text after text of photos of my grandmother. In one sepia-colored picture, she was seated next to my eldest aunt, smiling. I could see myself in her full cheeks, in her smile. I started to cry. Her name was Lucille. Light.

And there were more. Photos of my grandmother with other grandchildren. Photos of my aunt and her husband, my uncle. I did not know it then, but I had hundreds of aunties, uncles, and cousins just on my father's side. My grandmother was one of twelve children who survived to adulthood. She had been born in the Mississippi Delta, to church-going folks. Her father—my Granddaddy Harrison—had been a pastor. My grandmother, from a very young age, had lived a hard life. Eventually she fled rural Mississippi for Chicago, and then Springfield, Massachusetts. The second child born to her was my father.

Waves of awe swept over me. Here was connection, lineage, knowing my grandmother's name and what she looked like, the place from which my people came. Here was the first link to roots into a family that was *my* family. And that was not all. I was immediately mirrored in numerous ways. The second cousin who had put together an extensive family tree was a practicing Buddhist! She had my book on Black Buddhists on her shelf when the investigator reached out to her. I shared 3.93 percent of my DNA with her. She celebrated being connected to me.

Even now, rereading these words brings tears to my eyes. I had never, ever, had the experience of being claimed by family. It was profound. I have been able to attend family gatherings, even a family reunion. I have been able to visit my great-grandparents' graves near Leland, Mississippi.

On the day I visited my great-grandparents' graves, at the Holly Grove Missionary Baptist Church, it was 93 degrees outside. The sky was clear and blue.

My great-grandparents were buried in a segregated graveyard. Crabgrass grew over their headstones. But I could make out my great-grandfather's name and my great-grandmother's beside his.

I felt tremendous pride in their survival. I thought of Baldwin's words to his nephew: "You come from sturdy, peasant stock [that] . . . in the teeth of the most terrifying odds, achieved an unassailable and monumental dignity. You come from a long line of great poets."[6] I thought of what I had learned just two months prior to my trip. My great-grandparents had been born in the late 1800s and had raised twelve children. My great-grandfather had been a pastor and an organizer. I felt enormous gratitude for being part of their lineage.

I brushed crabgrass away from their graves. I tucked in flowers. In the distance, a riding mower hummed.

It is from this place of intertwined lineages—of Baldwin and Lorde, of Buddhism and my Black family members—that I now move. It is from this place of inner stability that I am able to hold space for the little sangha that meets weekly in my home, that I am able to protest with others against the ethnic cleansing of Palestine and the human rights abuses taking place in our own country. These are perilous times. And yet. By metabolizing our suffering, by dreaming and embodying our collective mother-warrior visions, we embody power. Unshakable authority.

Notes

Introduction

1 James Baldwin, *Go Tell It on the Mountain* (1952; Vintage Books, 1981), 1.

2 Baldwin wrote: "She [John's mother] did not know why he so adored things that were so long dead; what sustenance they gave him, what secrets he hoped to wrest from them. But she understood, at least, that they *did* give him a kind of bitter nourishment, and that the secrets they held for him were a matter of his life and death." Baldwin, *Go Tell It on the Mountain*, 167.

3 James Baldwin, "An Interview with James Baldwin," Studs Terkel, 1961, Conversations with James Baldwin (University Press of Mississippi, 1989), 5–6.

Chapter 1: The Transformation of Silence into Language and Action

1 Audre Lorde, "The Transformation of Silence into Language and Action," in *Sister Outsider* (The Crossing Press, 1984), 42.

2 Audre Lorde, "A Litany for Survival," in *The Collected Poems of Audre Lorde* (W. W. Norton, 1978), 31–32.

3 Benjamin E. Sax, *Israel, Antisemitism, and the Fate of Interreligious Dialogue: Definitions, Encounters, Hopes* (Bloomsbury, forthcoming), 56.

4 Many Buddhist practitioners of South West Asian and North African (SWANA) ancestry, as well as Jewish Buddhists, have challenged the complicity of mainstream, predominantly white Buddhist organizations and *sanghas*. *Gaza: Calling for a Dharma Response*, a zine published by an international coalition of dharma teachers, leaders, sangha members,

and organizations, published April 27, 2024, https://alokavihara.org
/wp-content/uploads/2024/05/Gaza-Calling-for-a-Dharma-Response
-updated-april-27-2024.pdf. See also *The Arrow: A Journal of Wakeful
Society, Culture, and Politics* 11, no. 1 (Winter 2024).

5 Lorde, "Transformation of Silence," 42.

6 James Baldwin, *The Fire Next Time* (Vintage Books, 1963), 36.

7 Baldwin, *The Fire Next Time,* 37.

8 Quoted in Keith P. Feldman, *A Shadow Over Palestine: The Imperial Life
of Race in America* (University of Minnesota Press, 2015), ix.

9 James Baldwin, *Conversations with James Baldwin,* eds. Fred L. Standley
and Louis H. Pratt (University Press of Mississippi, 1989), 86.

10 Nadia Alahmed, "'The Shape of Wrath to Come': James Baldwin's Rad-
icalism and the Evolution of His Thought on Israel," *James Baldwin
Review* 6, no. 1 (2020), 28–48.

11 Michael Fischbach, *Black Power and Palestine: Transnational Countries
of Color* (Stanford University Press, 2018), 9–29; 73–76.

12 See Baldwin, *Conversations with James Baldwin,* 86. There are many
definitions of Zionism. For a nuanced understanding of the term, see
Omri Boehm, *Haifa Republic: A Democratic Future for Israel* (New York
Review Books, 2021).

13 James Baldwin, "Open Letter to the Born Again," *The Nation,* September
29, 1979, www.thenation.com/article/society/open-letter-born-again/.

14 Sasha Polakow-Suransky, *The Unspoken Alliance: Israel's Secret Relationship with South Africa* (Pantheon Books, 2010); Ilan Pappe, *Israel and
South Africa: The Many Faces of Apartheid* (Zed Books, 2015).

15 These racialized social hierarchies in Israel are perpetuated more than
seventy-five years after the founding of Israel as a nation-state, even though
Arab and African Jews make up approximately half of the Israeli population. See Judy Maltz, "Ugandan Jews Not Eligible to Immigrate to Israel,
State Informs High Court," *Haaretz,* January 25, 2021, www.haaretz.com
/israel-news/2021-01-25/ty-article/.highlight/ugandan-jews-not-eligible
-to-immigrate-to-israel-state-informs-high-court/0000017f-f23d-df98
-a5ff-f3bdeffe0000.

16 Jonathan Watts, "Karma for Everyone," *Rethinking Karma: The Dharma
of Social Justice,* 2nd ed. Jonathan Watts (International Network of

Engaged Buddhists, 2014), 24. See also Nagapriya, *Exploring Karma and Rebirth* (Windhorse Publications, 2004), 14, 41–51.

17 Nagapriya, *Exploring Karma and Rebirth*, 33.

18 Nalin Swaris, "Karma: The Creative Life Force of Human Beings," in Watts, *Rethinking Karma*, 59.

19 Swaris, "Karma: The Creative Life Force," 41. Swaris is indebted to J. G. Jennings, translator and editor of *The Vedantic Buddhism of the Buddha: A Collection of Historical Texts* (Oxford University Press, 1947).

20 Swaris, "Karma: The Creative Life Force," 77–78, 122.

21 Swaris, "Karma: The Creative Life Force," 57–59.

22 Jessica Zu, "Collective-Karma-Cluster-Concepts in Chinese Canonical Sources: A Note," *Journal of Global Buddhism* 24, no. 2 (2023), 90.

23 Nalin Swaris, "Karma: The Creative Life Force," 52.

24 Ouyporn Khuankaew, "Buddhism and Domestic Violence: Using the Four Noble Truths to Deconstruct and Liberate Women's Karma," in Watts, *Rethinking Karma*, 200–24.

25 Swaris, "Karma: The Creative Life Force," 62.

26 James Baldwin, "Negroes Are Anti-Semitic Because They're Anti-White," in *The Price of the Ticket: Collected Nonfiction 1948–1985* (Beacon Press, 1985), 434.

27 For an extensive analysis of this point from a twenty-first century Jewish perspective, see Ben Ratskoff, "Against Analogy," *Jewish Currents*, June 9, 2020, https://jewishcurrents.org/against-analogy.

28 Baldwin, *The Fire Next Time*, 96.

29 Noel Ignatiev, *How the Irish Became White* (New York: Routledge, 2009).

30 Baldwin, "Negroes Are Anti-Semitic Because They're Anti-White," 434.

31 Baldwin, "Negroes Are Anti-Semitic Because They're Anti-White," 432.

32 Baldwin, "Negroes Are Anti-Semitic Because They're Anti-White," 436.

33 Baldwin, "Open Letter to the Born Again."

34 nyle fort, Marc Lamont Hill, Daniel May, Chandra Prescod-Weinstein, and Ben Ratskoff, "Reading Baldwin After Kanye: A Conversation about James Baldwin's 1967 Essay, 'Negroes Are Anti-Semitic Because They're Anti-White,'" *Jewish Currents*, September 28, 2023.

35 Baldwin, "Negroes Are Anti-Semitic Because They're Anti-White," 437.

36 Baldwin, "Negroes Are Anti-Semitic Because They're Anti-White," 437.

37 Right Thought and Right Speech are two parts of the Noble Eightfold Path, a core Buddhist doctrine.

38 Thich Nhat Hanh, *Vietnam: Lotus in a Sea of Fire—A Buddhist Proposal for Peace* (Hill and Wang, Inc., 1967), 88.

39 Martin Luther King Jr. "Beyond Vietnam—A Time to Break Silence," speech delivered at Riverside Church, New York City, April 4, 1967, www.americanrhetoric.com/speeches/mlkatimetobreaksilence.htm.

40 Thai Nghiem, "Our Way Out Is the Way In," in *Peace Begins Here: Palestinians and Israelis Listening to Each Other* (Parallax Press, 2004), 12.

41 See also Michael Krass, "Note to Reader," in *Gaza: Calling for a Dharma Response*, 8.

42 James Baldwin, "Stranger in the Village," in *The Price of the Ticket*, 100.

43 Mairav Onszein, "On Israeli Apathy," *New York Times*, October 7, 2024, www.nytimes.com/2024/10/07/opinion/on-israeli-apathy.html.

44 James Baldwin, quoted in *I Am Not Your Negro,* a film by Director Raoul Peck, from "Director Raoul Peck: James Baldwin Was 'Speaking Directly to Me,'" *NPR: Fresh Air*, February 14, 2017, https://www.npr.org/transcripts/515196224.

45 "Application of the Convention of the Prevention and Punishment of the Crime of Genocide in the Gaza Strip (South Africa v. Israel)," International Court of Justice, accessed December 13, 2024, https://www.icj-cij.org/case/192.

46 "'You Feel Like You Are Subhuman': Israel's Genocide Against Palestinians in Gaza," Amnesty International, December 4, 2024, amnestyusa.org/reports/you-feel-like-you-are-subhuman-israels-genocide-against-palestinians-in-gaza/.

47 Times of Israel Staff, "Data Shows Post-Oct 7 Emigration Surge from Israel, Which Has Since Stabilized," *Times of Israel*, July 19, 2024, https://www.timesofisrael.com/data-shows-post-oct-7-emigration-surge-from-israel-which-has-since-stabilized/.

48 The organizations Jewish Voice for Peace and IfNotNow have taken active, urgent stands against the genocide in Gaza.

49 Coalition of Dharma Teachers, "Gaza: Calling for a Dharma Response."
    An inactive Instagram account, "Buddhists 4 Justice in Palestine," also
    made this point.

50 Guiding Teachers Council, "Guiding Teacher Reflections on War &
    Nonviolence," Spirit Rock, May 15, 2024, https://www.spiritrock.org
    /articles/guiding-teacher-reflections-on-war-violence.

51 Rashid Khalidi, *The Hundred Years' War on Palestine: A History of Settler
    Colonialism and Resistance,* 1917–2017 (Macmillan Publishers, 2021).

52 Rashid Khalidi and Itay Mashiach, "Rashid Khalidi: 'Israel Has Cre-
    ated a Nightmare Scenario for Itself. The Clock Is Ticking,'" *Links:
    International Journal of Socialist Renewal,* December 10, 2024, https://
    links.org.au/rashid-khalidi-israel-has-created-nightmare-scenario
    -itself-clock-ticking.

53 Suheir Hammad, *Born Palestinian, Born Black & the Gaza Suite* (Univer-
    sity of Arkansas Press, 2012). Hammad's book was originally published
    by Harlem River Press in 1996.

54 Imani J. Jackson, "How Palestinian Protestors Helped Black Lives
    Matter," *USA Today,* July 1, 2016, www.usatoday.com/story/opinion
    /policing/spotlight/2016/07/01/how-palestinian-protesters-helped-black
    -lives-matter/85160266/.

55 Russell Rickford, "'To Build a New World': Black American Internation-
    alism and Palestine Solidarity," *Journal of Palestine Studies* 48, no. 4, 192
    (Summer 2019): 522–68; Fischbach, *Black Power and Palestine*; Keith
    Feldman, *A Shadow Over Palestine: The Imperial Life of Race in Amer-
    ica* (University of Minnesota Press, 2015); Angela Y. Davis, "Angela
    Davis: Standing with Palestinians—Reflecting on the Past 60 Years,"
    Hammer&Hope 3 (Spring 2024), https://hammerandhope.org/article
    /angela-davis-palestinians-gaza.

56 Ta-Nehisi Coates, *The Message* (One World Press, 2024).

57 Willa Blythe Baker, "Breaking the Silence on Sexual Misconduct,"
    Lion's Roar: Buddhist Wisdom for Our Time, accessed February 28, 2025,
    https://www.lionsroar.com/breaking-the-silence-on-sexual-misconduct/;
    Katy Butler, "Encountering the Shadow in Buddhist America," *Common
    Boundary Magazine,* May/June 1990, www.katybutler.com/author

/articles/encountering-the-shadow-in-buddhist-america/; Lama Rod
Owens, "#MeToo and the Guru," in *Love and Rage: The Path of Liberation Through Anger* (North Atlantic Books, 2020), 162–76; Ann Gleig,
"Sexual Violations in American Buddhism: Interpretive Frameworks
and Generative Responses," *Ten Thousand Things*, March 5, 2020,
http://blog.shin-ibs.edu/sexual-violations-in-american-buddhism
-interpretive-frameworks-and-generative-responses/.

58 Guiding Teachers Council, "Guiding Teacher Reflections on War &
Nonviolence."

59 This question is echoed by Sara Shapouri, "Neutrality Is an Illusion," in
Coalition of Dharma Teachers, *Gaza: Calling for a Dharma Response*,
34–39.

60 James Baldwin, "The Negro After Watts," *Time*, August 27, 1965.

61 The very suggestion of a "bi-national" state in which Arabs and Muslims
would have full rights, and perhaps even be in the numerical majority,
is still heard as deeply threatening for many Jews who called themselves
"pro-Israel" and advocate for a Jewish state. I hear this fear. But I do not
support any ethno-nationalist state.

62 My political stance is not specific to Israel; it includes the United
States, which actively incarcerates and controls the movements of six
million individuals—the vast majority of whom are people of African
descent—at any point in time. See Skylar Hathorn, "The Never-Ending
Sentence: How Parole and Probation Fuel Mass Incarceration," *The
Conversation*, April 2, 2025, https://theconversation.com/the-never
-ending-sentence-how-parole-and-probation-fuel-mass-incarceration
-250578. The US system of mass incarceration is a form of social control extending from more than two centuries of chattel slavery, Black
Codes, convict leasing, and Jim Crow segregation. For decades, I have
actively sought to dismantle it. I extend my activism to South Africa, a
country in which I lived and worked for two years, for the same reason:
The apartheid system, in all of its iterations, is anathema to me personally and ethically.

63 Lama Rod Owens, *The New Saints: From Broken Hearts to Spiritual
Warriors* (Sounds True, 2023), 170–72.

Chapter 2: Pain That Saves Your Life

1 James Baldwin, "Notes of a Native Son," in *The Price of the Ticket* (Beacon Press, 1985).

2 James Baldwin, "Introduction: The Price of the Ticket," in *The Price of the Ticket*. Baldwin wrote that white people embraced whiteness at the expense of their cultural heritage.

3 Baldwin, "Notes of a Native Son."

4 David Leeming, *James Baldwin: A Biography* (Arcade Publishing, 1994), 34.

5 Audre Lorde, "Poetry Is Not a Luxury," in *Sister Outsider* (The Crossing Press, 1984), 36.

6 James Baldwin, *The Fire Next Time* (Vintage Books, 1963), 4.

7 Baldwin, "Notes of a Native Son," 138.

8 Baldwin, "Notes of a Native Son," 138.

9 Baldwin, *The Fire Next Time*, 7.

10 Baldwin, *The Fire Next Time*, 8.

11 Baldwin, *The Fire Next Time*, 99.

12 "Audre Lorde," 1982 interview by Claudia Tate, reprinted in *Black Women Writers at Work*, ed. Claudia Tate (Continuum, 1983), 92.

13 "Audre Lorde," 1982 interview, 16.

14 "Audre Lorde," 1982 interview, 16.

15 Audre Lorde, "The Uses of Anger," in *Sister Outsider*, 135.

16 Audre Lorde, "Learning from the Sixties," in *Sister Outsider*, 142.

17 Lorde, "Eye to Eye: Black Women, Hatred, and Anger," in *Sister Outsider*, 146.

18 Lorde, "Eye to Eye," 171–72.

19 Lorde, "Poetry Is Not a Luxury," 36–37.

20 Lorde, "Poetry Is Not a Luxury," 37.

21 Baldwin, *The Fire Next Time*, 98–99.

22 Valerie Mason-John (Vimalasara), *Detox Your Heart: Meditations for Healing Emotional Trauma* (Wisdom Publications, 2017), 54–55; Vozdra, "Gabrielle Roth & The Mirrors—Percussion Through 5 Rhythms," YouTube, September 7, 2013, https://www.youtube.com/watch?v=PpX5JHYnT1M.

Chapter 3: Sun in a Sunless Place

1 Audre Lorde, *A Burst of Light* (Firebrand Books, 1988), 79.

2 Audre Lorde, *The Cancer Journals* (1980; Penguin Books, 2020), 8.

3 Lorde, *Cancer Journals*, 1.

4 Lorde, *Cancer Journals*, 4.

5 James Baldwin, "The Creative Process," in *The Price of the Ticket: Collected Nonfiction 1948–1985* (Beacon Press, 1985), 322.

6 Baldwin, *The Fire Next Time* (Vintage Books, 1963), 92.

7 Lorde, *Cancer Journals*, 5.

8 Lorde, *Cancer Journals*, 4.

9 Lorde, *Burst of Light*, 120.

10 Lorde, *Burst of Light*, 116.

11 Lorde, *Burst of Light*, 60–61.

12 Lorde, *Burst of Light*, 121.

13 Lorde, *Burst of Light*, 96.

14 Lorde, *Burst of Light*, 134.

15 Lorde, *Burst of Light*, 121.

16 Lorde, *Burst of Light*, 54.

17 Lorde, *Burst of Light*, 125.

18 Lorde, *Burst of Light*, 126.

19 "Upajjhatthana Sutta: Subjects for Contemplation."

20 Alexis Pauline Gumbs, *Survival Is a Promise: The Eternal Life of Audre Lorde* (Farrar, Straus and Giroux, 2024), 136–39.

21 Lorde, *Burst of Light*, 131.

22 Lorde, *Burst of Light*, 79.

23 Lorde, *Burst of Light*, 132.

24 James Baldwin, *Nobody Knows My Name* (Dell, 1961), 90.

25 Angela Y. Davis, *Freedom Is a Constant Struggle: Ferguson, Palestine, and the Foundations of a Movement* (Haymarket Books, 2016).

26 Baldwin was diagnosed with esophageal cancer in 1987. The cancer later spread to his liver.

27 Lorde, *Burst of Light*, 99, 100–101, 116.

28 See David Leeming, *James Baldwin: A Biography* (Arcade Publishing, 1994), 378–86. "The Welcome Table" is the name of a play that Baldwin conceived of and began writing in the last few years of his life.

29 "Feeding Your Demons® Online Program," Tara Mandala: International Buddhist Community, accessed February 9, 2025, https://www .feedingyourdemons.com.

Chapter 4: It Comes from Somewhere

1 James Baldwin, "On Being White . . . and Other Lies," *The Cross of Redemption: Uncollected Writings*, ed. Randall Kenan (Vintage International, 2010), 166–70.

2 Baldwin attempted to write a screenplay on the life of Malcolm X, a project that never came to fruition as he came up against the white norms of Hollywood; see also Nikole Hannah-Jones, *The 1619 Project: A New Origin Story* (One World, 2021), xvii.

3 James Baldwin, *Giovanni's Room* (Transworld, 1963).

4 James Baldwin Interview with David Estes, in *Conversations with James Baldwin*, eds. Fred L. Standley and Louis H. Pratt (University of Mississippi Press, 1989), 280.

5 The "white problem" is a phrase employed by Baldwin in a 1964 speech. See James Baldwin, "The White Problem," *Cross of Redemption*, 88–97.

6 James Baldwin, *The Fire Next Time* (Vintage Books, 1963), 19.

7 Baldwin, "No Name in the Street," in *The Price of the Ticket* (Beacon Press, 1985), 520.

8 Baldwin, "The Nigger We Invent," in *The Cross of Redemption: Uncollected Writings*, ed. Randall Kenan (Vintage International, 2010), 118.

9 Baldwin, "In Search of a Majority," in *Price of the Ticket*, 239–40.

10 David M. Oshinsky, *Worse Than Slavery: Parchman Farm and the Ordeal of Jim Crow Justice* (Free Press Paperbacks, 1996), 28.

11 Baldwin, *Fire Next Time*, 18–19.

12 Baldwin, *Fire Next Time*, 98.

13 Baldwin, "Notes of a Native Son," in *Price of the Ticket*. See also, "James Baldwin Comes Home," in Standley and Pratt, *Conversations with Baldwin*, 161.

14 Baldwin, "Of the Sorrow Songs: The Cross of Redemption," in *Cross of Redemption*, 124.

15 Baldwin, "Speech from the Soledad Rally," in *Cross of Redemption*, 100.

16 Baldwin, "Alas, Poor Richard," in *Price of the Ticket*, 294.

17 Baldwin, "On Language, Race, and the Black Writer" in *Cross of Redemption*, 114.

18 See, for example, James Baldwin, "Of the Sorrow Songs," 145–53.

19 Baldwin, *Fire Next Time*, 95.

20 Baldwin, *Fire Next Time*, 99.

21 Baldwin, "The Black Scholar Interviews James Baldwin," in *Conversations with Baldwin*, 150–51.

22 Baldwin, "An Interview with Studs Terkel," in *Conversations with Baldwin*, 17.

23 Baldwin, "James Baldwin—Reflections of a Maverick," in *Conversations with Baldwin*, 227.

24 In the *Rice Seedling Sutra*, Maitreya speaks to the venerable Sariputra, a disciple of the Buddha. While atop Vulture Peak Mountain, Maitreya and Sariputra are surrounded by 1,250 gods, demi-gods, divine beings, and humans. Maitreya gives an account of "causes and conditions" and speaks at length about how external conditions affect all that arises, and how internal conditions likewise affect consciousness, dispositions, and suffering.

25 Emily McRae, "White Delusion and Avidya: A Buddhist Approach to Understanding and Deconstructing White Ignorance," in *Buddhism and Whiteness: Critical Reflections*, ed. George Yancy and Emily McRae (Lexington Books, 2019), 43.

26 Bhikkhu Analayo, "Consciousness and Dependent Arising," *Insight Journal* 46 (2020), 56.

27 Charles W. Mills, *The Racial Contract* (Cornell University Press, 1997), 18.

28 Baldwin, "The White Problem" in *Cross of Redemption*, 90.

29 Baldwin, "The White Problem" in *Cross of Redemption*, 95–96.

30 James Baldwin, "We Can Change the Country," in *The Cross of Redemption*, 60–61.

31 Steve Biko, *I Write What I Like* (HarperSanFrancisco, 1978), 22–23.

32 Baldwin, *The Fire Next Time*, 91–92.

33 James Baldwin, "We Can Change the Country" in *Cross of Redemption*, 60–61. See also "A Conversation with James Baldwin," in *Conversations with Baldwin*, 45.

34 James Baldwin and Malcolm X Debate, 26:48–27:44, September 5, 1963, www.youtube.com/watch?v=sVNVb7sKwoU.

35 RAIN practice was first conceptualized by Insight teacher Michelle McDonald, who articulated the acronym and sequencing of the meditation practices. RAIN practice was later evolved by Insight teacher Tara Brach, who substituted the term "Non-attachment" with the word "Nurture." See https://www.tarabrach.com/blog-two-versions-of-acronym-rain/. In my own practice over time, I have combined the two approaches to conceptualize N-RAIN as a practice that starts with Nurturing and concludes with Non-attachment.

Chapter 5: Training Anger with Accuracy

1   Audre Lorde, "The Uses of Anger," in *Sister Outsider* (The Crossing Press, 1984), 130.

2   Lorde, "Uses of Anger," 127.

3   Alice A. Keefe, "Tending the Fire of Anger," *Buddhist-Christian Studies* 39 (2019), 68.

4   Audre Lorde, "Eye to Eye: Black Women, Hatred, and Anger," in *Sister Outsider*, 145.

5   Lorde, "Uses of Anger," 127.

6   Myisha Cherry, *The Case for Rage: Why Anger Is Essential to Antiracist Struggle* (Oxford University Press, 2021).

7   Myisha Cherry, "On James Baldwin and Black Rage: A Moral Psychology of Anger," Conceptual Foundations of Conflict Project, YouTube, October 28, 2022, https://www.youtube.com/watch?v=5JfpGenZUns. Cherry uses the term "anger" interchangeably with "rage."

8   James Baldwin, "Notes of a Native Son," in *The Price of the Ticket* (Beacon Press, 1985), 143.

9   James Baldwin, "Sonny's Blues," in *Going to Meet the Man* (Dell, 1957), 122.

10 Baldwin, "Sonny's Blues," 120.

11 Cherry, "James Baldwin and Black Rage."

12 James Baldwin, *Blues for Mister Charlie* (Dell, 1964).

13 James Baldwin, *If Beale Street Could Talk* (Signet, 1974).

14 Cherry, "James Baldwin and Black Rage."

15 Lorde, "Eye to Eye," 145.

16 Audre Lorde, "The Uses of Anger: Women Responding to Racism," in *Sister Outsider*, 131.

17 Anita Barrows, "The Light of Outrage: Women, Anger, and Buddhist Practice," in *Buddhist Women on the Edge: Contemporary Perspectives from the Western Frontier* (North Atlantic Books, 1996), 53.

18 Barrows, "Light of Outrage," 54.

19 Audre Lorde, "Uses of Anger," 127.

20 Audre Lorde, "Age, Race, Class and Sex: Women Redefining Difference," in *Sister Outsider*, 116.

21 Lorde, "Age, Race, Class and Sex," 116.

22 Audre Lorde, "An Interview with Audre Lorde" by Ilona Pache and Regina-Maria Dackweiler (1987) in *Conversations with Audre Lorde*, ed. Joan Wylie Hall (University Press of Mississippi, 2004), 167.

23 Lorde, "Age, Race, Class and Sex," 119.

24 Alexis Pauline Gumbs, *"We Can Learn to Mother Ourselves": The Queer Survival of Black Feminism, 1968–1996* (PhD diss., Duke University, 2010), 11.

25 Lorde, *Conversations with Lorde*, 167.

26 Lorde, "Age, Race, Class and Sex," 115.

27 Lorde, "Uses of Anger," 127.

28 Lorde, "Age, Race, Class and Sex," 119.

29 Lorde, "Age, Race, Class and Sex," 119.

30 Lorde, *Conversations with Lorde*, 24.

31 Alexis De Veaux, *Warrior Poet: A Biography of Audre Lorde* (W. W. Norton, 2004), 159.

32 Audre Lorde, *Zami: A New Spelling of My Name—A Biomythography* (Crossing Press, 1982), 157.

33 Elizabeth Alexander, "'Coming Out Blackened and Whole': Fragmentation and Reintegration in Audre Lorde's *Zami* and *The Cancer Journals*," *American Literary History* 6, no.4 (Winter 1994): 697.

34 Lorde, *Zami*, 195.

35 De Veaux, *Warrior Poet*, 159.

36 Lorde, "Age, Race, Class and Sex," 120–21.

37 Audre Lorde and James Baldwin, "Revolutionary Hope: A Conversation Between Audre Lorde & James Baldwin," *Mosaic Literary Magazine* 39 (2016): 42–52.

38 James Baldwin, *Notes of a Native Son* (Beacon Press, 2012), 97–98.

39 Baldwin, *Notes of a Native Son*, 140.

40 Baldwin, *Notes of a Native Son*, 139.

41 Lorde, "Eye to Eye," 152.

42 Lorde, "Eye to Eye," 146.

43 Lorde, "Eye to Eye," 146.

44 Lorde, "Eye to Eye," 168.

45 Lorde, "Eye to Eye," 169–70.

46 Lorde, "Eye to Eye," 171.

47 De Veaux, *Warrior Poet*, 241.

48 Lorde, "Eye to Eye," 173.

49 Lorde, "Eye to Eye," 174.

50 Barbara O'Brien, "The Metta Sutta: A Beloved Buddhist Teaching," Learn Religions, July 29, 2017, https://www.learnreligions.com/the -metta-sutta-450129. The Vajrayana Buddhist tradition is replete with references to the Great Mother. Buddhist scholar Judith Simmer-Brown describes the Great Mother, who in Vajrayana Buddhism is said to be powerful because of her distinctive capacity to express the vast, limitless (and genderless) nature of emptiness. (*Dakini's Warm Breath: The Feminine Principle in Tibetan Buddhism*" (Shambhala Press, 2002), 84–89. In an unpublished paper, Jae Carey described the writings of Tsongkhapa, a fourteenth-century Tibetan Buddhist scholar, which contain a practice known as "Recognizing All Beings as Our Mothers." This practice fosters cultivating relative *bodhicitta*—heart energy—"at first through the ground of affection, recognition of the kindness of mother beings, and the sincere wish to repay them, which leads to love." (Jae Carey, "Recognizing All Beings as Our Mothers: Reflections on Mother-Practice Journeys and Bodhicitta," Union Theological Seminary, May 2023.)

51 Simmer-Brown, *Dakini's Warm Breath*, 115.

52 Ruth King, *Mindful of Race: Transforming Racism from the Inside Out* (Sounds True, 2018), 150–53.

Chapter 6: Once You Have Light

1 James Baldwin, *Giovanni's Room* (Penguin Books, 1956); Suzanne Roszak, "Sex, Diaspora, and the New 'Italian Novel': James Baldwin's *Giovanni's Room* and Bernnard Malamud's *Pictures of Fidelman*," *Arizona Quarterly* 71, no. 4 (Winter 2015): 81–106.

2 James Baldwin, *The Fire Next Time* (Vintage Books, 1963), 42–43.

3 Audre Lorde, "The Master's Tools Will Never Dismantle the Master's House," *Sister Outsider* (The Crossing Press, 1984), 111.

4 Audre Lorde, "Uses of the Erotic: The Erotic as Power," in *Sister Outsider* (The Crossing Press, 1984), 54–55.

5 Lorde, "Uses of the Erotic," 55.

6 Audre Lorde, *Conversations with Audre Lorde*, ed. Joan Wylie Hall (University Press of Mississippi, 2004), 64.

7 Lorde, *Conversations with Audre Lorde*, 75.

8 Audre Lorde, *The Black Unicorn: Poems* (W. W. Norton and Company, Inc., 1978), 120–21.

9 Alexis De Veaux, *Warrior Poet: A Biography of Audre Lorde* (W. W. Norton and Company, Inc., 2004), 159.

10. Lorde, *The Black Unicorn*, 12.

11 Audre Lorde, "The Winds of Orisha" in *Undersong: Chosen Poems Old and New*, rev. ed. (W. W. Norton, 1992), 93.

12 Lorde, *Conversations with Audre Lorde*, 147.

13 Lorde, *The Black Unicorn*, 119.

14 Kara Provost, "Becoming Afrekete: The Trickster in the Work of Audre Lorde," *MELUS* 20, no. 4 (Winter 1995): 45.

15 Ayodele Ogundipe, as quoted in Provost, "Becoming Afrekete," 47.

16 Alexis De Veaux, *Warrior Poet: A Biography of Audre Lorde* (W. W. Norton, 2006), 147.

17 Audre Lorde, *Zami A New Spelling of My Name: A Biomythography* (Crossing Press, 1982), xvi.

18 Provost, "Becoming Afrekete," 47.

19 Provost, "Becoming Afrekete," 52–53.

20 Judy Grahn, quoted in Provost, "Becoming Afrekete," 46.

21 Provost relying on Herskovits in "Becoming Afrekete," 46.

22 In *Zami*, the lover Afrekete is the mother of a seven-year-old child.

23 Lorde, *Conversations with Audre Lorde*, 62.

24 Lorde, *Zami*, xv.

25 Lorde, *Zami*, 223.

26 Anh Hua, "Audre Lorde's *Zami*, Erotic Embodied Memory, and the Affirmation of Difference," *Frontiers: A Journal of Women Studies* 36, no. 1 (2015): 129–130.

27 AnaLouise Keating, "'Making Our Shattered Faces Whole': The Black Goddess and Audre Lorde's Revision of Patriarchal Myth," *Frontiers: A Journal of Women Studies* 13, no. 1, (1992): 31.

28 Audre Lorde, "An Open Letter to Mary Daly," in *Sister Outsider*, 66–71.

29 Audre Lorde, "The Master's Tools," 111.

30 Audre Lorde, *Conversations with Audre Lorde*, vii.

31 De Veaux, *Warrior Poet*, 154. De Veaux writes: "Lorde felt Ouidah was the spiritual center of Dahomey, and more than any other place in Africa, she felt that Dahomey was home. There, in the synthesis of Yoruba and Dahomean deities, she found what she believed was the religion of her foremothers and her spiritual connection to them. She found Seboulisa, the goddess of Abomey (once the inland capital of ancient Dahomey), who was worshipped as 'the mother goddess of all.' She found Oshumare, the Yoruba rainbow-snake deity, who signified unity between aggression and compassion. Oshumare was also known as *Da Ayido Hwedo* to the Fon people of Dahomey, for whom the deity signified the union of female and male energies and was sometimes represented as a pair of twins. She learned of Oboto, the sea-goddess, *Yemoja-Oboto* to the Yoruba. She found Mawu-Lisa, the highest deity of the Fon, whose combination of female (*Mawu*) and male (*Lisa*) aspects represented the union of the Moon and the Sun as a Fon ideal." (De Veaux, *Warrior Poet*, 151).

32 Lorde, *Conversations with Audre Lorde*, 148–149.

33 Alexis Pauline Gumbs elaborates this statement in her essay, *We Can Learn to Mother Ourselves: The Queer Survival of Black Feminism, 1968–1996* (PhD diss., Duke University, 2010).

34 Lama Thubten Yeshe, *Introduction to Tantra: The Transformation of Desire* (Wisdom Publications, 2014), 17–18.

35 Yeshe, quoted in Jan Willis, "A Vision of What Could Be: An African
    American Professor of Buddhism Looks at Race, Class, and American
    Dharma," *Tricycle*, Spring 2020. The full quote is as follows: "According
    to Buddhist tantra, we remain trapped within a circle of dissatisfaction
    because our view of reality is narrow and suffocating. We hold onto a
    very limited and limiting view of who we are and what we can become,
    with the result that our self-image remains oppressively low and ordi-
    nary conceptions of ourselves and then, from the empty space into
    which these concepts have disappeared, arise in the glorious light body
    of a deity: a manifestation of the essential clarity of our deepest being.
    The more we train to see ourselves as such a meditational deity, the less
    bound we feel by life's ordinary disappointments and frustrations. This
    divine self-visualization empowers us to take control of our life and
    create for ourselves a pure environment in which our deepest nature can
    be expressed. . . . It is a simple truth that if we identify ourselves as being
    fundamentally pure, strong, and capable we will actually develop these
    qualities, but if we continue to think of ourselves as dull and foolish, that
    is what we will become. The health of body and mind is primarily a ques-
    tion of our self-image. Those people who think badly of themselves, for
    whatever reasons, become and then remain miserable, while those who
    can recognize and draw on their inner resources can overcome even the
    most difficult situations. Deity-yoga is one of the most profound ways of
    lifting our self-image, and that is why tantra is such a quick and powerful
    method for achieving the fulfillment of our tremendous potential."

36 Yeshe in Willis, "A Vision of What Could Be," 111.

37 Peter Harvey, *An Introduction to Buddhism: Teachings, History and Prac-
    tices* (Cambridge University Press, 2013), 180. Harvey writes, "Tantric
    practice centres on the ritual evocation, especially through the use of
    mantras and visualization, of deities that are seen as in some sense
    awakened. . . . The emphasis on power and efficacy can be seen as a
    development of the idea of meditative psychic powers, which was there
    from the beginning in Buddhism."

38 Yeshe, *Introduction to Tantra*, 112–13. Tibetan Tantric Buddhism fol-
    lows an elaborate structure for deity yoga. The practitioner takes

refuge in the Three Jewels: the Buddha, the Dharma, and the Sangha. While taking refuge, the practitioner cultivates bodhicitta: motivation to achieve enlightenment for the benefit of others. The next step is to engage in guru yoga, which is visualizing the Tantric guide as embodying qualities that one wishes to cultivate in oneself, and ultimately, through visualization, merging with the guru's clarity and compassion. The third step in deity yoga is to meditate on bodhicitta–one's compassionate motivation—which fosters the arising of the deity in one's mind.

39 Audre Lorde, "Power," in *The Black Unicorn*, 108–9.

40 Provost, "Becoming Afrekete," 55.

41 Audre Lorde, *A Burst of Light*, 76–77. See also Elizabeth Alexander, "'Coming Out Blackened and Whole': Fragmentation and Reintegration in Audre Lorde's *Zami* and *The Cancer Journals*," *American Literary History* 6, no. 4 (Winter 1994): 697, 701.

42 Lorde, *Conversations with Audre Lorde*, 163.

43 Lorde, *Conversations with Audre Lorde*, 164.

44 Jan Willis, "Dakini," in *Dharma Matters: Women, Race, and Tantra* (Wisdom Publications, 2020), 174.

45 Judith Simmer-Brown, *Dakini's Warm Breath: The Feminine Principle in Tibetan Buddhism* (Shambhala Publications, Inc., 2002), 42.

46 Justin Miles, *Sadhana of Awakened Melanin: Black Power Meditation Liturgy* (Published by Author, 2020), 10–13.

Chapter 7: Personal Power That Moves Us

1 James Baldwin, *The Fire Next Time* (Vintage Books, 1963), 9.

2 Andre Kaczynski, Jennifer Hansler, and Em Steck, "Trump Appoints Speechwriter Fired for Attending Conference with White Nationalists to Top State Department Role," CNN, Monday, February 3, 2025.

3 Kaczynski, Hansler, and Steck, "Trump Appoints Speechwriter."

4 Kaczynski, Hansler, and Steck, "Trump Appoints Speechwriter."

5 Kamilah Majied, *Joyfully Just: Black Wisdom and Buddhist Insights for Liberated Living* (Sounds True, 2024), 21.

6 Baldwin, *The Fire Next Time*, 10.

Acknowledgments

Writing this book has been a tremendous act of discovery. During this process, I was able to connect to my paternal family of origin. I learned of my great-grandparents, Rev. Benjamin Harrison Gordon and Mallie Fox Gordon, and my grandmother, Lucille Gordon Green. I am moved to tears when I recall the depth to which I have been embraced by my grandmother's descendants: my aunts and uncles, and literally hundreds of cousins. When I reached out to learn more about my father's people, I had no expectations for how I would be received. Their warmth has been deeply fulfilling. I am especially grateful to my cousin Shundrea Trotty, who has done extensive genealogical research of the Gordon family and who brought me into the fold, and to my aunt Brenda Green, who always lets me know that she is thinking about me. I am moved by all of the family members who reached out after my home city of Asheville suffered a hurricane in September 2024.

I also celebrate my spiritual grandmothers—Rev. Dr. Annie Ruth Powell and Thea Jackson—who embodied what it meant to make a way out of no way. They loved me fiercely and believed in my capacity to endure, indeed thrive. I thank my godmothers, Via Wynroth and Judi Lejeck, who served as mother-figures while I came of age. And I lift up Dr. James H. Cone, who saw in me an ability to produce innovative scholarship, born out of my struggles to "achieve an identity," as Baldwin would say. Dr. Cone was the first to encourage my academic writing life.

More recently, I have been blessed to be supported in unfathomable ways. First and foremost, I am grateful to Shakiyla Smith-Sengu and Rodney McKenzie Jr of the Fetzer Institute. I am moved to tears yet again when I think of the degree to which they have championed my work. I am eternally grateful to the Rev. Alicia Forde for making what has been a life-changing introduction. I also thank my agent Mark Tauber, who saw the possibility of this project when it was still a fledgling idea. I am grateful to my acquisitions editor, Jasmine Respess at North Atlantic Books, who stood firmly behind my desire to write a chapter about the genocide in Gaza and offered unlimited support as I worked through many, many drafts. I also thank my production editor, Trisha Peck, and my copy editor, Rebecca Rider, whose careful readings made the manuscript much stronger. Finally, I thank my writing coaches Vanessa Zuisei Goddard and Sebastian Matthews, who offered critical encouragement as I shifted this book from an academic analysis of Baldwin and Lorde to a deeper, more personal encounter with their lives.

I embrace all of the aforementioned persons as part of a support system. I am blessed to be part of a nationwide Black Buddhist community that continues to coalesce as we prioritize connection with one another. Many of these community members—teachers, practitioners, and writers—have inspired this book as they have quoted Baldwin and Lorde in their dharma talks and publications and on their websites. In the summer of 2021, I taught an online class entitled "The Dharma of James Baldwin and Audre Lorde" through the Barre Center for Buddhist Studies. It was lovely to be in conversation with likeminded souls. I later co-published an article, "Awakening Through Audre Lorde," in *Lion's Roar* magazine with my dharma sisters Leslie Booker, Pamela Ayo Yetunde, and Aishah Shahidah Simmons. Their insights into the dharma teachings of Audre Lorde provoked in me a deeper encounter with Lorde's writings. I am also grateful for the reflections of my interlocutors—especially Ruth King, Michelle Alexander, Toni Pressley-Sanon, Ralph Craig III, Kaira Jewel Lingo, and Valerie Mason-John (Vimalasara)—as well as the Buddhist teachers of Deep Time Liberation, a retreat that inspired my journey to find my father's people. I uplift Noliwe Alexander, DaRa Williams, Devin Berry, and Rosetta Saunders for their guidance.

I thank the many teachers and Buddhist organizations that allowed me to incorporate into this book practices that have been deeply meaningful for me: Lama Rod Owens, Ruth King, and Sounds True; Karla Jackson-Brewer and Pieter Oosthuizen of the Tara Mandala-International Buddhist Association, and Justin Miles.

As I worked out many of the ideas presented in this book, and did a sustained dive into Baldwin's and Lorde's essays, I had the great fortune to teach graduate students at Union Theological Seminary over three semesters. I loved every moment of it. I was deeply inspired by the creativity of the students, including their conversations, weekly responses, and final essays. It was by far the best experience of teaching in the classroom that I have ever had.

I also recognize the extensive support of my colleagues in Buddhist Studies, and in Black Religious Studies more broadly. I thank Jonathan Gold, who invited me to join Princeton University's Center for Culture, Society, and Religion as a Visiting Affiliate Fellow while I completed this manuscript. I am also grateful for the friendship of Ann Gleig, Nalika Gajaweera, Sarah Jacoby, and Ralph Craig III, whose work in Buddhist Studies inspires my own. I thank Judith Weisenfeld and Tracey Hucks, whose efforts to support scholars of Black Religious Studies have fostered my initiatives for reaching beyond the academy.

I uphold Palestinian and Jewish scholars and practitioners who have helped me evolve a Buddhist Social Ethical response to the genocide in Gaza. I especially thank Kareem Ghandour and Benjamin Sax for helping me think through the nuances of the genocide and making themselves available to process hard questions. I thank the community of pro-Palestinian spiritual activists that gathered in February 2025, just as I was finishing revisions, and the hosts of the Watershed Center in upstate New York, who so generously offered a space to write in the final stretch.

I am deeply, deeply grateful to the editors of *The Arrow* journal—including Kareem—who published an issue on a Buddhist response to Gaza just as I was completing my chapter on collective karma. It came at exactly the right time.

I uplift friends and family near and far for their ever-present support. I thank Letitia Campbell, Jermaine McDonald, Francesca Morfesis, Keaton Hill, and Dawn Chavez for their constant encouragement. I am grateful to members of an emerging little sangha here in my hometown of Asheville, especially Ekua Adisa, Isissa Komada-John, Kris Moon, Cassandra Lam, Ambar Olivarez, Justin Tucker, and Christina Torres. My sister-in-law Kris Lewis offered tremendous support as she assisted me in the early stages of genealogical research and helped me figure out a way forward. My mother and stepfather have also been a constant source of support, particularly with child care and housing, as we have tried to discern how to raise a family in the midst of my various projects.

I am filled with deep gratitude for my family's love. I uplift the steadiness and blessings offered by my spouse Ethan, who has provided boundless support for nearly two-and-a-half decades. He supports my writing process even when it makes family life difficult. We celebrated twenty years of marriage with a trip to Paris—a journey inspired by Baldwin—while I was writing this manuscript. And always, I am in awe of my two kiddos. Maathai, now a teenager and an artist, appreciates the groundbreaking paths walked by Baldwin and Lorde when being Black and queer was marginalized, indeed penalized. And Jaxson, who loves to grow fresh food and encourages me to eat it, still insists that I get on the floor to play every day.

Permissions

Practices

Index

About the Author

Rima Vesely-Flad, PhD, is the author of *Black Buddhists and the Black Radical Tradition: The Practice of Stillness in the Movement for Liberation* (NYU Press, 2022) and *Racial Purity and Dangerous Bodies: Moral Pollution, Black Lives, and the Struggle for Justice* (Fortress Press, 2017). She is the founder of the Initiative for Black Buddhist Studies and the recipient of grants from the Fetzer Institute, the Henry J. Luce Foundation, the Fredrick P. Lenz Foundation, the Crossroads Program, and the US Department of State Fulbright program. You can follow her work at www.blackbuddhiststudies.org and on Instagram @blackbuddhiststudies.

About North Atlantic Books

North Atlantic Books (NAB) is an independent, nonprofit publisher committed to a bold exploration of the relationships between mind, body, spirit, and nature. Founded in 1974, NAB aims to nurture a holistic view of the arts, sciences, humanities, and healing. To make a donation or to learn more about our books, authors, events, and newsletter, please visit www.northatlanticbooks.com.